ALSO BY SUE WILLIAM SILVERMAN

Because I Remember Terror, Father, I Remember You
(Winner of the Associated Writing Programs
Award Series in Creative Nonfiction)

LOVE
SICK

One Woman's
Journey Through
Sexual Addiction

Sue William Silverman

W. W. NORTON & COMPANY

New York · London

Copyright © 2001 by Sue William Silverman

For information about permission to reproduce selections from this
book, write to Permissions, W. W. Norton & Company, Inc.,
500 Fifth Avenue, New York, NY 10110

The text of this book is composed in Berling Roman with the
display set in Locarno Italic
Composition by Molly Heron
Manufacturing by Haddon Craftsmen Inc.
Book design by Charlotte Staub
Production manager: Julia Druskin

Library of Congress Cataloging-in-Publication Data

Silverman, Sue William.
Love sick : one woman's journey through sexual addiction /
by Sue William Silverman.
p. cm.
ISBN 0-393-01957-8
1. Silverman, Sue William. 2. Sex addicts—United States—Biography.
3. Sex addiction—Case studies. I. Title.

RC560.S43 S56 2001
616.86—dc21
[B]   00-069250

W. W. Norton & Company, Inc., 500 Fifth Avenue,
New York, N.Y. 10110
www.wwnorton.com

W. W. Norton & Company Ltd., Castle House,
75/76 Wells Street, London W1T 3QT

1 2 3 4 5 6 7 8 9 0

To Marc Sheehan

for his poetry and grace

When sex is used for the wrong reasons
a spiritual problem is created.

CHARLOTTE DAVIS KASL

Was it doubted that those who corrupt
their own bodies conceal themselves?

WALT WHITMAN

ACKNOWLEDGMENTS

A VERY SPECIAL THANK YOU to my agent, Wendy Weil, for her belief in this book and her wise counsel.

I am honored to have Carol Houck Smith as my editor at W. W. Norton. Her unerring editorial vision and wisdom guided this book to its completion.

Michele Orwin is my valuable first reader and lifelong friend.

Malcolm Call, editor of my first book, is an important friend. I value him for all the ways he continues to support me.

Christopher Noël, with insight, perception, and humor, greatly assisted this manuscript's evolution.

I am forever touched by the generosity of David Bradley.

My amazing therapist taught me what I know about sobriety and safety. He never gave up on me, even when I gave up on myself. In these ways, he helped with the creation not only of this book but also of me.

I feel blessed that Ellen Jagolinzer and Mona Oppenheim have always been there for me . . . and blessed that Bryna Livingston, my role model, taught me so much about being an adult woman.

A permanent thank you to the Associated Writing Programs for all it does for me and so many other writers.

I WANT TO THANK the people who shared their stories and their lives with me during my journey through treatment. I must honor their right to privacy by changing their names and identities. In some instances, events have been reshaped and composite characters created in order to protect these and other individuals.

LOVE
SICK

LAST
DAY
OUT

EVERY THURSDAY AT NOON I have sex with Rick in room #213 of the Rainbow Motel. Today, even though I promised my therapist I wouldn't come here again, I pull into the lot and park beside Rick's black Ford Bronco. I cut the engine and air conditioner and listen to stillness, to nothing, to heat. Sunrays splinter the windshield. Heat from the pavement rises, stifling, around the car, around me. No insects flutter in the brittle grass next to the lot. Trees don't rustle with bird wings. A neon rainbow, mute and colorless by day, arcs over a sign switched to VACANCY. Only the little girl from India, daughter of the motel owner, invigorates the stasis. Holding a string tied to a green balloon, she races down the diving board and leaps into the swimming pool. With the windows closed, I can't hear the splash. If she laughs, I can't hear this, either. For a moment she disappears. The balloon gaily sways above the water. The girl pops to the surface. She begins the game again.

The girl's energy exhausts me—as much as the stagnation of neon, air, time. I close my eyes. Still, I sense no darkness, no cool shadows, no relief from the scorching Georgia heat. Rather, a harsh light, white as a sheet, penetrates my lids as if I am caught in an unforgiving glare.

I worry the girl by the pool will see me. She's too young to know what I do here in the Rainbow Motel.

I should leave. I should leave here now. I should drive home and rinse pink gloss from my lips, wipe mascara from my lashes, change out of my too-short skirt and too-tight black lace blouse. I should cook a nourishing dinner for my husband. I should grasp the balloon and let it waft me across the sky, far from my implacable need for men. Dangerous men. Not physically dangerous. Emotionally dangerous. These men see me just as an object, a body. They are men incapable of love—even though I endlessly, addictively, try to convince myself that sex at noon for an hour with a married man *has* to be the real thing, must be love.

So I can't leave here. I need Rick. One last time. One last high. One last fix.

I should drive to the rehab unit and find my therapist right now.

Pausing outside the door of room #213, I hear the television: a car crash, urgent voices. I turn the knob and lock it behind

me. Rick lies on the sheet smoking a cigarette, the remote
beside him. He inhales. Exhales. Smoke swirls. I watch it dis-
perse. An ash drifts onto the pillowcase. He doesn't notice.
He hasn't stopped watching me since I entered.

He leans over and stubs out the cigarette. He clicks off the
television and beckons me closer. A gold necklace nestles in
his blond hair, a rich glitter of gold on gold as if chain mail
emblazons his chest. Lying beside him, I curl short strands of
his hair around my finger as if, in all this incandescence, we
radiate love. His Eau Sauvage cologne is the only scent in the
world I will ever need or want. I close my eyes, drenched in
it. In him. I must feel Rick's touch, a drug surging through
veins, trancing me as I urgently swallow oblivion and ether.
Sex, a sweet amnesiac. The elixir drains through my body,
thin as a flame. I crave this, need him—or You, Man, whoever You are—until I'm blissfully satiated. . . .

Is this bliss?

I open my eyes. He's leaning over me, his palm on the pillow beside my head. I can hear the second hand of his watch
ticking beside my ear. His breath numbs the hollow at the
base of my neck. Sweat gathers on his temples. The necklace
taps my chin as he fucks me. A gift from his wife? I wonder.
He kisses me. Strokes me. But this is just a repetition of all
the other times with Rick. Nothing unusual. Just the basics.
Routine sex. He doesn't even bother to try to impress me
with fancy positions like Crushing Spices. Flower in Bloom.
Dear to Cupid. Just the missionary position. Sometimes
sixty-nine—but all Rick wants is to get the job done.
Quickly.

Not that I mind. *I don't do this for pleasure. I do this for love.*

Except I feel a damp chill between my shoulder blades—thinking of all the times my spine has creased this mattress—so many mattresses. The second hand ticks. He pushes up on his elbows, his head above mine. He glances down, focusing more on my torso than on me. I hug him tighter. Feel *me*. See *me*. I touch his throat with the tip of my tongue. His skin tastes like salt water and indigo. My limbs feel weighted with leaden male gravity. Smothered. I feel as if I sink below water, far beneath a night sea.

Can't I understand that this, what we do here, has only, ever, been numbed emotions of familiar strangers, fucking? Why can't I accept the difference between this and love? How can love be two bodies wrapped in a sheet that's singed by careless cigarettes, here, in a room with plastic curtains, tin ashtrays, base metal, stained carpet, bad alchemy, artificial air, and a television promoting the same pornographic movies every hour on the hour? Here in a room when, by one o'clock, Rick looks depleted, the blue of his eyes seeming to have bled beneath the skin.

Rick retrieves a Polaroid camera from a small gym bag. He aims it at me, still lying in bed, my head propped on the pillow. He jokes: "Smile." I stare straight into the lens. In the flash I am dazed, as if I've imploded.

I know he needs this photo like a stash, a memento, in order to remember while I'm gone.

Tomorrow morning I am to enter an inpatient treatment facility where I must remain sexually sober for twenty-eight long days. I don't want to go. But if I don't, I'll remain addicted to sex, to men, to dangerous men. My therapist, whom I've been seeing for almost a year, says I must go. For out here, loose in the world, I haven't been able to stop on my own.

Rick goes to shower.

Pieces of my body surface in the Polaroid. My neck down to my knees. I want to be pleased. For only when my body is desired do I feel beautiful, powerful, loved. Except I *don't* feel powerful, loved, or whole now. I feel shy, embarrassed, exhausted. Less. Yes, as if I am less than a body. For right now my body seems to exist only in this Polaroid.

For months, like a mantra, my therapist has told me, "These men are killing you." I don't know if he means emotionally, spiritually, or physically. I don't ask. He explains that I confuse sex with love, compulsively repeating this destructive pattern with one man after another. I do this because as a girl I learned that sex is love from my father, the first dangerous man who sexually misloved me.

"I thought the intensity with Rick *must* be love," I say.

"The intensity is an addict's 'high,'" my therapist says. "Not love." To numb the shame and fear associated both with the past and with my current sexual behavior, I medicate, paradoxically, by using sex, he explains. "But sometimes that 'high' stops working. Usually after a scary binge."

Like last Thursday at Rick's house.

Rick and I didn't meet at the Rainbow Motel. His son was home from school with the flu, and Rick took the day off from work to stay with him. Rick and I undressed in the bedroom he shares with his wife, while his son slept in his room down the hall. The house was hushed. The door to the bedroom locked. But then I heard a small sound: his son crying.

Rick heard him, too. I expected Rick to rush to him. We wouldn't have sex. Instead, we would read his son a story. *I* wanted to read his son a story. Give him a glass of water. *I* wanted to give him a glass of water. Press a washcloth to his cheeks. I paused, sure I felt his son's fever, damp and urgent. He needed his father.

His father didn't need him.

Rick's hands tugged at belts and zippers: hurry. We *will* do this . . . even though his son might get out of bed, knock on the door, see me leave his parents' bedroom. What I then forced myself to know was that *this*, this one careless act of sex, was more important to Rick than his son. And because I, too, couldn't say no, because I feared Rick would leave me if I refused him sex, I began to know, had to accept, that sex was more important to me, too. In a moment of clarity I realized that, while the sober part of me wanted to attend his son, a tangled, humid, inescapable part stopped me. Time stalled: with Rick's hands forever on his belt buckle; with my fingers always on the zipper of my skirt.

And a moment later, I no longer heard his son crying.

The next therapy session I told my therapist, Ted, about

Rick's son. More: I confessed that I'd been secretly meeting Rick for weeks without telling him, Ted. I couldn't stop. Before I'd left Ted's office, he called the inpatient unit where he worked and scheduled my admittance. He told me it wasn't possible for him to work with clients who showed up for a session "drunk" or "hungover." He could no longer see me as an outpatient; he could only help me in the rehab unit. "To have *real* feelings, you have to be sexually sober," he said. "Not numbed out." Afraid to be abandoned by Ted, beginning to accept the emotional destructiveness of my behavior, I agreed to go.

Now, as I cross the motel parking lot, dingy afternoon light fuses my blouse to my sweaty back. All I want is to sleep it off. My footsteps sound hollow. My mouth tastes contaminated, metallic. The little girl and her green balloon are gone. Without her energy, the pool is a flat, glassy sheen. Driving from the lot, I pass the neon sign, silently spelling RAINBOW MOTEL.

I should never return here; yet I can't imagine not meeting Rick every Thursday at noon. For what I do in room #213 is the only reason, I believe, a man would love me . . . *what my father taught me was love.*

That evening my husband and I eat a silent dinner at the kitchen table. Andrew sits erect, solid, focused on a Braves baseball game on the portable television, while I hunch over my plate. Andrew takes angry bites of an overdone hamburger, the third one I fixed this week, and canned string beans, all I managed to prepare after returning from the motel. I nibble at an edge of hamburger and spear one bean onto my fork. I put it down without eating. Looking at all the food, I think I might be sick. Fumes from the motel seem to rise from the hem of my skirt. My body feels sticky and smudged. It feels unhealthy. Andrew seems not to see, pretends not to notice, this mess that is me. Or, yes, he notices. But he never asks questions. He is too afraid of the answers.

"Sorry about the dinner," I say.

He isn't angry about the affairs; he doesn't know about them. He's angry about my emotional disarray. He wants me to be industrious and smiling. Normal. I worry, even with therapy, I won't learn how to love him the way I should, won't learn how to act like a wife.

"I was wondering," I say, during a television commercial break, "maybe you could drive me over there tomorrow and help me get settled."

"I can't just not teach my classes." His fingers grip the fork.

I want to touch his hand, loosen the grip, warm our fingers.

"I need to finish grading papers." He pushes back his chair. "Remember to call your parents, tell them where you're going," he says. His six-foot body fills the doorway. "I wouldn't know what to say if they call here looking for you."

I scrape my uneaten hamburger and beans into the garbage. Nothing to clean from Andrew's plate, only a smear of ketchup, a few bread crumbs. I squeeze Ivory liquid soap onto the sponge and wash several days' worth of dishes. With a Brillo pad I scour the long-encrusted broiler pan. I sprinkle Comet in the stained sink. I set Andrew's blue cereal bowl on the counter next to his coffee mug, ready for his breakfast in the morning. I want to do more: mop linoleum, polish hardwood floors. I *want* to try harder to please Andrew. I never can. There's always a distraction, always a Rick, or someone. Now, tonight, I feel the burden of calling my parents, the burden of going to the hospital, press against my back. I feel as if I've lost all my muscles.

I turn on the lamp in the living room and sit on our Victorian couch. I pick up the telephone and dial my parents' number. My mother answers on the second ring. Even though my parents know I'm in therapy, I've never said the word *incest* aloud in their presence. Whenever I visit, once or twice a year, we still eat dinner on pretty Wedgwood plates the way we always did. We are silently confused with each other, or else we speak as if no one heard my father turn the doorknob on all my childhood bedrooms . . . never heard the door click shut all those nights.

Now I say to my mother that I have something important to tell her. There is a pause before she answers, "Sure, honey," then places her hand over the receiver. She calls to my father, who picks up the extension. "Hi, precious," he says to me.

I tell them there's nothing to worry about. I've just been depressed and need to go away for about a month. "I'll be at this treatment facility where my therapist works."

"I don't understand," my mother says. "I thought you said you've been doing so much better."

I have told them this lie. They are paying for my therapy sessions, and I want them to think they're getting their money's worth. Ironically, they want me to feel better even as they never ask why I need therapy in the first place.

"How do you know this therapist knows what he's doing?" my father says. "He doesn't know anything about you."

This therapist knows my life is out of control, I want to say. He knows I'm afraid to eat, can't feed my body. He knows I fuck men because it's what *you* taught me is love.

Father, this therapist knows *everything*. About you.

The back of my neck is sweaty, and I coil my hair around my fist. Quizzle, my cat, jumps on the couch and curls beside me.

I barely hear my voice. "He knows I don't know how to love right," I say.

"What kind of people would be in a place like that?" he says.

The more he speaks, the more weightless my head feels, the more sluggish my body. My stomach cramps: with hunger, with fear. I don't know if I can do this.

"People like *me*," I whisper.

"I won't hear about this," he says.

"Dad, wait. My therapist said he'll want to schedule a family session. I mean, I know you can't come down here, but we'll do it on the phone. Like a conference call."

"If he wants a meeting, tell him to send me an agenda."

"That's not exactly how it's done."

"Then how can I know what we're going to talk about?"

What do you think we're going to talk about?

The phone clicks.

I know we'll never have a family session, even on the phone.

"Mom?"

"I'm still here."

"You think he's really angry?"

"Can't you call him from the hospital *without* these therapists?"

My therapist has told me I'm to have no unsupervised contact with my father while in the hospital. No contact with Rick, either.

"How about I'll send you flowers?" she adds.

I don't want flowers. I don't want presents. All you give are presents. You gave *me* as a present. To your husband. By feigning illness and staying in bed, your eyes shut, the door closed, you could pretend not to notice how you made me available to your husband—a gift—a little-girl wife.

"Mother, I don't want flowers, I want . . ."

"What?"

The impossible: a real father; a mother who saw what she saw, knew what she knew. Even though the last time my father touched me sexually was when I left home for college some twenty-five years ago, it feels as if I've never left that home at all.

"Just to get better, I guess," I answer.

"Well, be sure to pack a warm robe and slippers," my mother says. "Bring plenty of vitamin C. You know how cold they keep those places." I am about to hang up when she adds, "Oh, and call your sister. She's doing so well in her new job."

I put down the phone and sink back into the velvet cushion on the couch. I grew up in pretty houses decorated with art objects my father bought on his many travels; how easily our family hid its secrets behind carved wood masks from Samoa, straw fans from Guam. How successful we seemed, with elegant tea sets from Japan, silk curtains from Hong Kong. Now Andrew and I have nice antiques, an Oriental rug, watercolor paintings. *Things.* I was raised to believe that if a family appears perfect, it must *be* perfect. I have tried to keep up appearances.

I open the door to Andrew's study. He doesn't look up. He is an English professor, and he sits at his desk grading student papers. I lean over his shoulder and wrap my arms around his chest. I tell him I called my parents, that my father hung up, that my mother worries I'll catch cold. He sighs, and doesn't put down his pencil.

I straighten and lean against his desk. Bookcases jammed with volumes by James Joyce, Thomas Pynchon, Tolstoy, Cervantes, Jane Austen, Derrida, Riffaterre, Kant, line the walls like thick insulation. He is writing a book of his own, evolved from his dissertation. I have typed the manuscript several times for him, several revisions. I have proofread it twice. Yet I only have a vague understanding of what it's about.

Even though I married Andrew for his cool distant silence—so different from my father's needy raging—now, this moment, I want to get his attention. I want to say: Look at me! I want to crack the silence of our marriage and reveal to him the *complete* reason my therapist says I must enter the hospital now: to be sequestered, quarantined, from men. But I can't tell Andrew. For I believe if he sees the real me, he'll leave me. All he knows for sure is that I'm entering treatment because what happened to me as a child caused an eating disorder and I hate food.

I turn, about to close the door to his study. "I'm sorry," is all I'm able to say. "You know?"

"Look, I'm sure it'll be fine," he says. "Call me when you get there. Let me know you made it okay."

Later I lie awake, where I sleep by myself, in a small second-story bedroom. The attic fan whooshes air from the basement up through the house and out the windows, out the vents in the gable. The house feels vacant. Andrew sleeps directly below me in a king-sized bed. I roll onto my stomach in my narrow bed and press my fingertips against the wood floor. I want to feel a quiet vibration from his breath. I want to tiptoe down the stairs and slip beneath the covers beside him. I want the scent of his freshly laundered sheets on my own body, his clean, strong hand to hold mine. I want to feel a reassuring, constant presence of this man labeled "husband." I don't know how. Ordinary married life is too tame and mild. I want to hold on to him, but Andrew, as well as our ten-year marriage, only skims the periphery of my senses.

Initially I moved in with Andrew because he asked me. I was searching for love, even though I was married to someone else at the time. But bored with my first marriage, I thought all I needed to be happy was to switch partners. After a divorce and living together about a year, Andrew and I decided to marry. The morning of our wedding, however, I awoke with a headache, my muscles stiff with the responsibility of maintaining a relationship: yes, too ordinary, committed, boring. Not as intense or exciting—not as short-lived—as a one-night stand or an affair. Scant weeks before the wedding I'd even come close to having sex with the president of a company where I was doing "temp" work for $4.50 an hour. I'm not sure why I said no to that president, except maybe this time I really wanted to make a stab at marriage.

I'd ordered my "wedding dress" out of a catalogue. It was a red cotton floral outfit, marked down to nineteen dollars.

Andrew urged me to buy something nicer. I couldn't.

How could I tell him I bought the dress because *I* felt marked down? How could I wear white or cream or tan when red is my true color?

Three-thirty in the morning. The silence of our house, our marriage, wells up around me. Night is a thick humid wall. I need a way out. I push back the sheet and retrieve a lavender wood box I've hidden for years in my closet. I sit on the floor. Inside the box is my stash—stuff hoarded for when I need a fix—these mementos of men almost as good as a real man. Letters, photos, jewelry, books, pressed flowers. A maroon cashmere scarf that an older married man gave me when I was a college student in Boston. I drape the scarf around my neck.

From my dresser I remove khaki shorts, underwear, socks, a few wrinkled T-shirts, a pair of gray sweats, and place them in my canvas suitcase. I slide my fingers along metal hangers in the closet. Short skirts. Silk and lacy blouses. Rainbow Motel blouses. I also own blazers and oxford shirts, professional clothes, from various past jobs, even though I am currently unemployed. Size-four dresses to clothe my anorexic body. Size-eight for when I'm eating. But little in this closet is appropriate for a hospital. On a shelf in the back I find an oversized white T-shirt with the stenciled message: STRANDED ON THE STRAND. It is so old the seams are splitting, the print fading. I bought it in Galveston, where I once lived, in an area called the Strand. I always read the message literally: I have felt stranded. Everywhere. I decide to wear it tomorrow.

I tuck the maroon scarf between the shirts in my suitcase.

Next to my bedroom is the bath. I collect deodorant, toothbrush, toothpaste, comb. No makeup. Not even lipstick for this new sober self I will try to create tomorrow. In the medicine cabinet is my supply of Gillette single-edged razor blades. Why not? The metal feels cool, comforting. The blades are to slice small cuts in my skin. How peaceful, whenever I drift into a trance of silver razors, obsessed with watching slivers of blood trail down my thighs. Small hurts always distract me from the larger hurts. Blood, starvation, promiscuity, are *managed* pain, meant to relieve larger, *un*manageable pain.

I slip a razor blade under the bar of Dove soap in my pink plastic soap dish and put it in my suitcase.

DAY
ONE

THE NEXT MORNING, when the door to the rehab unit shuts behind me, I feel trapped. I feel exposed in the shock of fluorescent light. I can't move. Away from the comforting silence of my room at home, there's too much noise and movement to comprehend what anyone is doing or saying. Women, a blur of voices and colors, rush down the hall. One woman, who must be anorexic, lags behind. She's bundled in heavy sweats to warm her emaciated frame, and pushes an I.V. pole on wheels, a bag of Ensure hanging from the prongs. A tube runs from the Ensure into her nostrils. It occurs to me: this is not a joke.

I step back and grip the doorknob. This place isn't for me,

it's for other women, far worse off than myself. After all, I only agreed to come here because Ted said I had to. I am about to back out the door when a man, his hair in a black braid, pries my canvas suitcase from my grasp and carries it away. A nurse propels me into the medical doctor's office.

I'm given a hospital gown, told to remove my clothes. Urine samples. Blood. My temperature is taken to see if I'm freezing to death like that anorexic woman. I'm told to stand on a scale, backward, so I can't see my own weight. My height is measured. I lie on an examination table and the nurse sticks suction cups to my chest for an EKG. I'm given a pelvic. I'm told to open my mouth. A wood stick is placed on the back of my tongue. I gag. To my empty stomach, even this tastes like food. They check for electrolyte imbalance. Dehydration. Traces of alcohol. Drugs. Cancer. Viruses. STDs.

Bone density tests. A mammogram. X rays.

Pictures of my body.

Don't bother, I want to say. That smutty Polaroid of my torso, inert on a bed, available, could tell them everything they want to know about ribs, spine, elbows, throat, knees— body parts I always believed equaled me.

I am handed forms to fill out: *What did you eat last night for dinner? What did you eat for breakfast? How many hours of sleep did you get last night?*

"Steak, potatoes, apple pie," I write in the first blank.

"Eggs, bacon, orange juice, cereal, hash browns, toast," I write in the second.

"8 hours," I write in the third.

My thin fingers can barely grasp the pen. I am shivering and want to ask for my sweatshirt, but I can't speak. I don't know how to ask where they've taken my suitcase.

When did you last have sex?

"This is a tough question," I write in the blank space.

How many sexual partners have you had in your lifetime?

I need a calculator. No, it's okay, I soothe myself. Lie. I decide to include just the men I saw more than once. The men I saw more than twice. The ones that at least gave the illusion of a relationship. I wonder if I'm supposed to count husbands. Do they mean my father? On the palm of my hand I begin to print names, counting. I write the number "15" in the blank. I cross it out. "10."

Have any of these sexual partners ever physically abused you or caused you pain? Do you ever use "props" such as whips or chains?

"Of course not," I write, pleased to find at least one question I can answer truthfully.

How do you define a sexual extramarital affair?

"LOVE," I write in the blank space.

When did you last menstruate?

I have no idea. Since I don't want to even consider the possibility of pregnancy, I pay no attention to cycles. I pay no attention to my body.

This isn't true.

I pay *intimate* attention to my body: decorating it, scenting it—a fantasy body created for fantasy men.

Rather, it is to *this* body I've paid no attention, the one here, now, under unrelenting lights. *This* body in a drab hospital gown is neither decorated nor perfumed. It is my real body here in the hospital that I don't understand: the one that looks plain and simple.

I write, "None of this matters," in the blank and put down the pen.

To come to the hospital today, I dressed this supposedly sober body in khaki shorts and the white STRANDED ON THE STRAND T-shirt. I yanked my curly auburn hair into a severe ponytail. I did not bother to tie the laces of my red leather Reeboks. Now when I finish filling out the forms, I put on these clothes again and sit by the door. The nurse returns with my Gillette single-edged razor in a plastic bag. Like evidence at the trial of a guilty defendant. I now realize that the man with the black braid had taken my suitcase to search it.

"That's just to shave my legs," I say to the nurse.

She pauses before speaking. I know she knows I'm lying. "They can go without being shaved for twenty-eight days," she says.

I lower my lids, ashamed. Under the fluorescent light I cast no shadow. This unit, me, my body: we are all being blanched by truth.

She hands me a sheet of paper. "Unit Guidelines." *Rules?* Quickly I skim it . . . *must be with a "buddy" at all times, no overeating, no starving, no vomiting, no masturbating, doors to rooms must be kept ajar, must participate in all groups and activities, no Spandex tights, no leotards, no tank tops, no smoking, no caffeine, no sugar, no antacids, no vitamins . . .*

"My mother told me to bring my vitamins," I say.

"*We'll* give you what you need here," the nurse says.

She points me toward the group room, where I'm to meet Ted, my therapist. I walk alone to the end of the hall.

I slouch in a wing chair across from Ted. We are alone in the lounge furnished with ordinary pink and gray uphol- stered couches and armchairs, lamps with white shades, gray industrial carpet. Prints of butterflies are hung on the walls.

Ted waits for me to speak. Even with the door shut, I hear laughter and voices in the corridor. Even with windows closed, I hear traffic rumble along the parkway. How can I speak in this confusion of sound? I wonder if I can remain mute for twenty-eight days. I don't know what to say. Even after months of therapy, I struggle to trust this most trust- worthy man I know—in his ordinary blue shirt, blue slacks, white Nikes, his hair the color of warm copper. His sky blue eyes are clear, honest, neither dangerous nor mysterious. His truth is basic, straightforward: stay sober; stay safe.

"How's it going so far?" His voice is both firm and gentle.

"They searched my suitcase."

Ted's pen makes a scratching sound as he writes on his yellow legal pad. "What did they find?"

I shrug. "I wish it could be like before. Seeing you out there." I nod toward the window.

"You weren't doing too well out there." Then he reminds me of the agreement I made the first time I saw him: if I relapsed, if I couldn't stop acting out my addiction with Rick, I would come here.

"How'd you get through yesterday?" he asks. "You see Rick?"

I pull up my legs and fiddle with the untied laces of my Reeboks. How can I explain I didn't want to see him? How can I explain I had to?

"I just keep hoping," I whisper, "that if only one of these times he would really love me, then everything would be okay."

"Except he—none of these men know how." Ted puts the cap back on the pen. "Sex addiction is a *misguided* search for love. And family."

Is that what I really wanted, I wonder, when I wanted to tell Rick's son a story rather than have sex with Rick: a family?

And then Ted tells me, patiently repeating what he's been telling me for weeks, that water seeks its own level, that sober people find sober people. Addicts find addicts—or they find codependents—who are addicted to addicts, who support the addict in their addiction. "Repeating this same pattern with these same men, over and over, isn't going to get you a different result."

He holds up a copy of a Workbook: *Addictions and Intimacy Problems*. The cover is decorated with blue butterflies like the ones in the prints on the walls. "Write about these men for your First Step," he suggests. "It'll help you see how this isn't about love, but about addiction."

Ted turns the Workbook to page one and hands it to me. "Let's see how you answer these questions."

In capital letters are the words: *WHEN SEX IS THE ANSWER TO EVERY QUESTION . . .*

Affirmative answers to these questions may mean an addiction to sexual behavior:

- Do you stay in unsatisfying, humiliating, or unhealthy relationships only so you can continue to have sex with someone?
- Do you fantasize about sex, masturbate, or use sex in any way in order to escape, deny, or numb your feelings?
- Do you believe that your sexual thoughts and behaviors cause problems?
- Does illicit sexual behavior hurt your ability to form an intimate relationship with a loving partner?
- Have you ever thought you might be cross-addicted to chemical substances, alcohol, or food?

I want to erase the questions in the Workbook. No: I want to erase the answers.

I stare across the room—not at Ted—rather, at nothing. Space itself seems to lighten to the color of frost, to dry ice numbing my brain. Cool and nonexistent. I'm unable to absorb this Workbook, this treatment center. This therapist.

"You're going to do all right here," he says. "Be patient with yourself. And start writing out your First Step." He nods at the Workbook.

I stand to go, but pause next to his chair. "I made a couple of mistakes on those forms they gave me."

He tells me he'll arrange for me to receive a new form.

"Go on back to the nurses' station," he adds. "Someone will take you to your room, introduce you to your roommate, Jill."

Jill? I don't want a roommate. I assumed I would be in a room all alone, just like at home. "Aren't there any singles?"

Ted shakes his head. "Addicts like isolation too much. And you need to learn to make some friends. Women friends. *Real* friends. Not men. Not addicts."

"Except everyone *here's* an addict."

"But you'll be working together, helping each other, to get better."

After dinner, I stand looking out the window in my room. Headlights and taillights rush past the hospital. They seem to move purposefully, cars driving toward family homes, lives, dinners: a kind of life and definite future I want, but don't know how to enter.

In the near distance, behind me, is the reflected image of my room, as anonymous as room #213 in the Rainbow Motel, although sterile rather than corrupt in its anonymity. Tan cinder-block walls, tan bedspreads, industrial carpeting.

But now I notice that a shadow has darkened the window's reflection, superimposed upon this present, that future. A man stands framed in the doorway watching me. He doesn't move, doesn't speak. I turn. I look straight at him. It's the same man who took my suitcase this morning. He's dressed in black denims and T-shirt. A rubber band secures his braid woven with a white feather.

He crosses the room and hands me another copy of that questionnaire. "Ted asked me to give you this," he says. I take a deep breath, about to speak. But he turns to leave. I want to touch his turquoise earring. I want to touch the wounded skin of the scar tracking his arm.

In the corridor, Jill, my roommate, passes the man—too close. I feel her dark, dazzling energy, like black neon at midnight. The man must sense this, too. He pauses. She glances at him before entering, her perfume dense as a contrail. Jill is both false and alluring—alluring because she *is* false, enticing as a decoy. Glossy brunette hair, red lips, dark-shaded eyes, crimson blush. Makeup designed for bars and motels.

Jill looks toward the man's disappearing back. She looks at me. "Gabriel," is all she needs to say.

Gabriel.

Her slow smile is professionally seductive. Not toward me. Not even necessarily toward Gabriel. Rather toward seduction as a generic concept. I sit on my bed and do not smile back. Jill sits before a desk cluttered with cosmetics, lotions, brushes. She studies herself in her makeup mirror encircled with pink light bulbs. I turn away from her, not wanting to see our two faces overlap in her mirror.

Gabriel is an aide, Jill tells me. He helps the nurses, organizes activities, drives the van. "Hardly a real therapist," she adds. With mascara removed from her left eye, her face has a slightly unbalanced appearance. "*He's* not off limits."

To Jill, I suspect, even if Gabriel were Freud, he wouldn't be off limits.

I pick up the Workbook that Ted gave me this morning: *Addictions and Intimacy Problems*. The subtitle states it is based on the 12-Step model and is suitable for sex addicts, love and romance addicts, alcoholics, compulsive eaters, compulsive starvers, compulsive gamblers, shoppers, code-pendents—whatever is one's drug of choice. We are all equal. I turn to the section "First Step for Addicts." It is a list of behaviors in which I may have engaged. I don't want to read them, fearing I may have engaged in them all. I am to list examples in the blank spaces. This scares me as well. For *I* have too many blank spaces that need filling. I've kept secrets since I was a child, all the secret men, my secret, dangerous father, my secret lives.

Do you lie about your sexual behavior? Has your behavior affected values or relationships? Spirituality? Do you feel shameful or empty after sex or sexual fantasies?

Only when denial no longer works.

I sigh and close the Workbook.

"Don't believe that stuff." Without makeup, Jill's face seems frail, almost perishable, in its human color. A beauty mark has vanished. Her real marks, freckles, sprinkle her nose and cheeks.

"But this place . . ." I nod at the spare, antiseptic room. Two metal beds with tan spreads, two metal desks with matching chairs, one vinyl easy chair pushed next to the window, two prints of butterflies in plastic frames—*more* butterflies. This long night, this endless month. How can I explain to Jill I want to be isolated in my dim room at home with my comforting obsessions, in familiar surroundings? Solitude. It is *here* I am lonely—even with a roommate, women, nurses, noise, activities. Who am I—who will I become—here, without those men? "I guess I don't know if I can make it," I say.

"Don't worry," she says. "There're ways around all the rules. I mean, they go through all the trouble to search us, but then don't even know enough to block outgoing calls. Or screen incoming calls, either." She points to the phone on the stand. "And you can't get AIDS from phone sex! Safest sex there is."

Rick. "So we can call whoever we want?"

"Just watch out for Ted," Jill says. "He knows our 'act.' But some of the nurses—dumb." She motions toward my Workbook and tells me not to worry about confessing my secrets when I write out my First Step, that the information is for ourselves, or to share with our roommates and "buddies." "I don't think the nurses even bother to check," she adds. "Which means you can leave it blank altogether—or write *porno*, for all they know."

"I haven't even thought about what to write yet," I say. "How long you been here?"

"Three days." She tells me that the staff at an alcohol and drug detox center referred her here after she slept with one of the other patients and tried to seduce her therapist. "Frankly, I wouldn't have come if I'd known all the patients here were women."

"Is that why you're interested in Gabriel?"

"I never met a stranger who *didn't* interest me," she says. "*Men.* The stranger, the better." Jill shakes a bottle of purple nail polish with silver glitter. "And *here*, Gabriel's about *it*. So I guess it's every girl for herself."

She dips the nail polish brush in the bottle and dabs off excess. She glides it across her left thumbnail, beginning with a stripe in the center. Her focus is intense, careful not to smudge polish onto the cuticles. She holds her hand to her mouth and blows against the nails, drying them.

Moments pass before I realize I am as engaged in the perfection of her nails as she is. Down the hall I now hear voices, music, a television. Jill appears unaware of the noise, unaware of me. She doesn't even seem aware that *she* is in the room.

In a way, she isn't. While she seems to focus on each finger, I suspect the part of her that's an addict fantasizes an evening of moonlit seduction. Men.

I, too, have imagined crimson nails against the tanned skin of a man . . . against white sheets, black sheets, silk sheets, cotton sheets.

Jill and I are fellow dreamers.

"That's better." Jill admires her nails. She nods at the bottle of polish, offering it to me casually, like a drink. "But I'm thinking I might check out early," she adds. "Ted's been messing with my mind."

Leave? This isn't a locked unit, Ted has told me. We committed ourselves here; we weren't committed. We can leave whenever we want.

DAY
TWO

IN A BLUR this first full morning, I stumble through the routine. Six A.M. wake-up. Half asleep, I stagger from bed to the scale in the nurses' station across from my room for weigh-in. Then back to our rooms to dress in sweats for exercise, out the (unlocked) double doors at the entrance to our wing of the hospital on the sixth floor. Wait for the elevator. Downstairs, we pass the information desk in the lobby and head outside. We circle the cinder-block-glass hospital, walking or jogging, for twenty minutes. Back in the elevator, sixth floor, turn right through the double doors again. Jill's and my room is the third one on the left. Shower (at least Jill and I have our own bathroom), then back downstairs to the cafeteria for breakfast. We're forced to eat everything placed on our trays by the nurse, even oatmeal, soggy with milk. Noise, rules, distractions, women, food. So used to slowly waking alone every morning and filling myself with thoughts of Rick, of men. Here I'm overwhelmed by chatter, radios, demands: *get out of bed, eat this food, don't be late to group.*

Twelve rooms open onto the one corridor that comprises our unit. The lounge, where we meet for group therapy at ten A.M., is at the far end, the same room with pink and gray upholstered chairs and couches where I met Ted yesterday. I claim a chair by the door, as far away from the others as possible—about fifteen women altogether. The woman with the I.V. pole on wheels, the bag of Ensure, sits by the window, her eyes shut. With her pale, wispy hair, in the glare of sunlight, she seems almost transparent.

One of the patients, Sheila, begins to speak, her voice reaching me, slowly, from across the room. I don't want to hear. I don't want to speak. I wish *I* could be transparent, unnoticed. Through partially lowered lashes I see Ted watch Sheila, just as he's watched and listened to me over the last several months in his outpatient office. He concentrates on his clients, understanding what we *really* mean, when we're unable to explain our truths or who we are. He teaches us *his* truths: honesty, safety, sobriety.

"What would it mean for you to learn to have sex in a loving relationship?" Ted asks Sheila, who insists she's not a sex addict, doesn't belong here, because she has never once had sex.

"I'd rather eat," she says. Sheila, her body disguised in

black baggy sweats, tugs at the ends of her brown, short-cropped hair. She licks her lips, which are pale, as if she swallowed all their color.

Maybe because I'm anorexic her body scares me—as if obesity is contagious. I don't understand why she starves her body sexually while overfeeding it with food. Maybe her addict self tricks her into believing her body doesn't need sex if it is satiated with food.

I imagine Sheila in her home wearing those black sweats. I imagine she eats so much she can't keep pace with the garbage, and her house is strewn with empty sacks of potato chips, empty boxes of Ritz crackers, stacks of crushed Coke cans, Twinkies wrappers, discarded cans of tuna, jars of peanut butter scraped clean. I imagine Sheila at midnight, suddenly waking, panicked to find herself all alone. She rushes to the kitchen and throws open cabinets. . . . Later, even as she staggers from the kitchen, she will always return to her bedroom feeling empty.

"So, what, you masturbate?" Jill smiles at Sheila, a tough lipsticked smile.

"How about a little respect?" Ted chides Jill.

"How come you tell Sheila to have sex and I'm supposed to stop having it?" Linda says to Ted. Linda, one of the other patients, sat across from me at breakfast this morning.

"Just stop the affair with your ex-boss," Ted says. He adds that then, sober, she will learn to be emotionally intimate with her husband, and sexually intimate with him, too.

"But all my married friends have affairs and think it's perfectly normal." Linda wears new-age hippie clothes of embroidered cotton with a silk shawl. "Besides, it's the only thing that makes me happy."

"Except you're confusing 'high' with 'happy,'" Ted says. "Don't you feel more lonely after?"

Linda nods. Tiny bells, sewn to the hem of her gypsy skirt, tinkle as she crosses her legs. "It's just when he and I are together, I feel so great. The hassles of marriage, kids—fall away."

Linda . . . what does *she* do at midnight? Maybe she wakens. Maybe she listens for the swish of tires whispering down her moonlit street. A lover. Approaching. She slips from bed, from her sleeping husband, her bedroom, her house, to meet him. Her lover, a man she will never know but a man she will forever desire, unravels her scarf like a groom lifting a veil. Tassels on her shawl undulate in the ripple of lake water, where she lies on the bank, listening to the insistent sound of tiny copper bells as he fucks her.

"How did things go with Andrew before you left?" Ted asks.

I pull up my legs and try to shrink back into the cushions. In the dry air-conditioning, my throat feels tight. I'm not used to being emotionally honest.

Speaking softly, I tell him Andrew and my father are both angry: that I'm in therapy, that I need to be hospitalized, that I'm a mess. And that my father refused to participate in a family session.

"Maybe they're angry that you're going to get better," Ted says. He makes a note on his yellow legal pad. "Your father must be terrified you're telling the family secrets." He pauses. "And Andrew—if *you* get better, he'll have to make some changes, too."

"You mean that 'water seeks its own level' thing?"

He nods. "I know Andrew is a nice guy. But if you become emotionally available, intimate, he'll have to learn to open up more to you, too. And not work all the time." Ted gestures toward his own head. "Or stay in his head." As opposed to his heart, Ted means.

Andrew. *Always*, it's hard for me to even think about him. . . . So many other men. "I just wish I *felt* as if I loved him as much as I feel like I love Rick," I say.

"Except *real* love isn't obsessive," Ted says.

"Suppose you're addicted *to* love?" Linda asks.

"Still an addiction," Ted says. "Don't give your power to your addict side. Don't let *it* make decisions about what's 'love.' Or anything else."

Ted asks us to open our Workbooks. *WHEN SEX IS THE ANSWER TO EVERY QUESTION* . . . He says we're to fill in the blank pages for our First Steps, write about the men with whom we acted out sexually. For only after we understand and resolve our pasts can we begin to really move forward and get better.

Jill drops her copy of the Workbook on the floor. "But sex *is* the answer to every question," she says. She tells us that when she was in tenth grade in Pensacola she fucked the crew of a Navy destroyer. While her voice exaggerates, her body and eyes tense: daring and challenging. "And there I was, looking for love, without my Trojan value pack."

"'Looking for love in all the wrong places . . .' sounds like."
Ted mimics the country-western song. "But since you're here
now, what would you think about letting this group offer
you the hope and experience you need for recovery?"

"Yeah, right," she says. "My only hope is fucking. The only
experience I have is fucking. And fuck recovery."

"No, *you* fuck recovery," Linda says. "It's not easy, but some
of us want to at least try."

Slowly Jill scuffs the spike heel of her shoe against the carpet. With every swing of her leg, her ankle hits the base of
the chair. "I'm really sick of this being ashamed of sex," she
says.

"Come on, Jill, quit acting out," Ted says.

"You want to see acting out?" She stands and takes one
step toward him. She reaches up and unbuttons the top button on her blouse.

"Stop it," Ted says. "Now." His voice is firm. He takes a
deep breath. "Maybe you were taught to act this way in your
family." Ted glances around the room, his gaze lingering on
each of us, waiting for us to look at him, too. "But here we
can learn to be a different kind of family. Without the addiction, you can learn real love. And friendship. Learn to be the
kind of 'sisters' each of you deserved and would have
wanted."

Jill's fingers move away from her blouse. She holds up her
hand, palm out. "*Sisters*," she says. "If the best you can offer is
another fucking sister, I'm out of here. Besides, who're you,
telling me what to do?"

"Someone who cares what happens to you," Ted says.

"Well, I don't care what happens to any of *you*."

After she leaves, the room seems too quiet. Ted writes another note on his pad.

"But I don't understand," I say finally. "What did you mean about 'sisters'?"

"There's power in the group," Linda answers. "We can help each other stay away from those men. Like whenever you want to call Rick, call *me* instead." She has a small dimple above the right side of her mouth that deepens when she smiles. "We'll talk about it until you don't want to call him. It's like how AA works. Except our 'alcohol' is sex."

"Once you learn, here, how to be with safe, emotionally available women," Ted says, "my guess is that you'll be more interested in safe men, too, when you leave here."

After group I return to my room. Jill's suitcase is on her bed, and she's tossing clothes into it. She has two additional suitcases, so this will take a while. Jill is too angry to speak. And while I'd like to say something to mollify her, I suspect she's too enraged to hear me, hear anybody. I sit on my bed, propped against the pillow, and open my Workbook to the First Step. But it's hard to ignore her. Her anger is as strong as a magnet, able to latch on to any object that enters its field.

Jill dumps makeup in plastic cases. She unplugs her radio and mirror. Scoops curlers into a zip-lock baggie. She is invincible, intrepid, in her addict's uniform of spike heels, black skirt, red silky blouse, makeup. The air is heavy with perfume, encapsulating armor. She pushes all three suitcases to the door. The harsh *sweep-sweep* of her stockings sounds like background music to her addict's rage.

She returns to her bed and yanks off the cards and photographs she taped to the wall. Rather than dump them in the trash, she tosses them onto the desk. Thinking she might come back? She doesn't, even once, glance at me. Her eyes, encircled with liner, are narrowly focused.

Again, like last night, our similarities scare me. I know what would happen to *me* out there; so I know what *will* happen to her. I want to tell her to wait, but I know she won't, can't, hear me—can't even hear herself.

"You know, maybe it'd be a good idea if you give me your phone number," I say. "Just in case."

The corners of her eyes tighten. With annoyance? I grab my pencil and scrawl the number she gives me in the margin of my Workbook. I know she won't repeat it. When I look up, she's gone.

I rush to the window. In a few minutes she appears in the parking lot lugging two suitcases, kicking the third, past a row of cars to a Miata. And even though I don't want to be in the hospital, either, still, seeing Jill actually *out there*, while also envisioning her later this evening cruising nighttime bars, I want to pound on the window, get her attention, and stop her.

It is too late to stop her.

Just as she lifts a suitcase into her car, a silver pickup pulls alongside her. Even before the driver opens the door, I know it is Gabriel. Jill turns. With a foot on the scuff plate and her knee bent, her skirt hitches up her thigh. On that asphalt parking lot, shimmering with heat, she is pure mirage. Just as a shaman's sacred costume acts as bait for spirits, so is Jill's wardrobe created as bait for a man.

Gabriel, dressed in black, removes a scrap of paper from a pocket. Jill searches her purse and hands him a pen. He writes something down. Her phone number.

I press my forehead hard against the window . . . as if he might see me, know I am here, and hear what I'm thinking.

I could make you happier than Jill. I'm willing to give you my number. I'm willing to give you much more.

WORKBOOK—FIRST STEP FOR ADDICTS

In the First Step we admit we are powerless over our sexual behavior. We use sex like drugs to relieve pain, loneliness, and anger. But the sex makes us feel even more depressed, empty and ashamed. So the cycle to numb our feelings begins again. . . .

Evenings, after dinner, from seven to nine, we're supposed to read sections of the eighty-three-page Workbook, fill out charts, list examples, admit, confess, divulge, reveal secrets and histories of addictive lives.

I flip through the Workbook, not sure how to get started.

When did you first realize you might have a problem?

Last week at Rick's house, with his sick son?

No. Earlier.

Almost a year ago, when I first began therapy with Ted, after what happened with that writer—that laureled, haggard writer of fictions.

I print his name in the blank space.

Wait. I erase it. He's more dangerous than the others. Too scary to write about him.

From Linda's room across the hall, I hear music. Elton John. "I'm Still Standing." A theme song, no doubt, for those who survive all twenty-eight days in the program. Twenty-six more to go. In the margin of the Workbook, I multiply 26 by 24 = 624 more hours.

I flip to page three. *List examples of your sexual behavior that show the unmanageability in your life.*

In that wooden lavender box I keep a photograph of me in my early twenties. I am at Ocean City, New Jersey. It is late winter. I stand under a boardwalk beside a thick supporting column. I wear a black leather jacket. My fist is clamped to my waist, my elbow juts. Self-consciously I look at the bold black graffiti carved into the wood column:

LOVE
IS
HERE
EVERY
DAY♥

A contradiction exists, however, between that pose in the black leather jacket and my shy smile.

So who am I really in the photo? Am I young, shy, as the smile suggests? Or am I a seductive slut, like the pose and jacket suggest? Both. The photograph is of me and of my addict, competing for space in one body.

Of course I know a man left the message. He left it for
me, for *my* body to stand beside. If he emerged from darkness beneath the boardwalk he could find me and lead me
wherever he wanted. For surely I am HERE for him EVERY
DAY! *I* am the word LOVE in the graffiti. I read that word
as if it's my name, a proper noun. I am his definition of love.
Your definition. I am any definition you desire.

One April night, when I'm a student at Boston University, I
am defined by a stranger who calls my dorm. He is the
stranger who translates the word *love* into "danger," the
stranger for whom I always wait. He is the stranger who
knows I will be the only one to answer the late-night phone
call in a girls' dorm.

The moment I say hello, he asks what I am wearing. He
whispers, "Tell me," into the phone.

Before I think to lie and entice with a silky nightgown, I
say, "Pajamas. Flannel. Blue."

"Unbutton them," he says.

"Okay," I say, although I don't. Weak, I sink onto the wood
chair and raise my knees under my chin.

"Meet me," he says. "I want to fuck you."

Yes, I think, pleased: this is what men always want to do to
me, what I want them to do.

His breath is harsh, anonymous, familiar.

"Okay," I say. "Maybe. When?"

"Tomorrow," he says. "Five o'clock. Halfway across the
Mass. Ave. bridge."

"What do you look like?" I say.

"What will you wear?" he asks.

What to wear on a first date with an obscene phone caller? "A red miniskirt," I answer.

"I'll find you."

We hang up. Neither of us asked the other's name.

The next morning I open the window to early spring. I feel slow heat, smell the Charles River, spongy and weedy, about to burst with life. All day I long to meet him on the bridge. And all day, like a con artist, I prepare for this job—reconfiguring clothes, hair, body, makeup. In this familiar trance, I don't notice lapses in my breathing. Applying crimson polish, I can't notice that the skin beneath my nails is lavender, like the core of ice.

The man waits for me on the bridge. I see him from several yards away, and I walk steadily toward him—this obscene phone caller with glasses and crew cut. "My dorm's just the other side of the river," he says when he greets me.

I nod, smiling shyly. I can be authentic and shy, the same smile as in the

LOVE
IS
HERE
EVERY
DAY♣

photograph.

But then it's as if I step from the border of that photograph and, in fraudulent clothes, speaking a vocabulary of false desire, I follow a path into the addiction. The farther we journey across the bridge toward Cambridge, the bolder, more spurious, is my expression. The trance, which I entered when I answered the phone last night, is a contagion. It is my own form of alexia—word blindness—a condition that causes me to define words, as well as men, in order to fit the needs of my addict. So now I am able to believe he meant to call *me*, this was not a random obscene call.

We enter his dorm room. The bed is unmade. Dirty clothes smell slightly sweaty, yet exhale lust. He lights a candle—for romance, I want to believe—even as I know, once he draws the curtains, it is for darkness. For we would not want to see each other's faces. No longer do I even remember how he looked crossing the bridge. His thin body is obscure, his face pale and unhealthy. We are vague, indistinct, lethal.

He sits on a chair and tells me to take off my clothes. I do. I must. I must be desired. My body is shaved, lotioned, perfumed, decorated with makeup and beads and glitter. I unbutton my blouse, but it is the chambers of my heart that seem to have snaps, snapping open, releasing a rush of blood. My fingers glide down the zipper of my skirt, the tips icy. But I believe I am aglow in candlelight, my breath tongues of flame to caress him, seduce him with shaman powers. I am nude. He trails hungry hands along my body and nudges me onto the bed. He kisses me. I hold on to his shoulders and close my eyes. Because I feel no real emotions, I manufacture artificial ones. I seek comfort in this kind of sex I call love, which is all I know—all I've been taught—even as I *don't want* to know this. Yet, paradoxically, I can only distract myself from this knowledge by having more and more sex.

After, he drapes a lifeless arm across my stomach. From outside in the hallway, I hear a group of students talking about physics, the tangible world, real life.

Returning alone, recrossing the bridge over the Charles River, I imagine myself atop the rail. I clasp the hem of my red skirt, a parachute, and float down to the river. I sink underwater. Deeper. I slip below surfaces to the past. Where dark passageways lead to childhood bedrooms . . .

. . . the one on Southern Avenue in Washington, D.C. I am four and live in a white house across from a cemetery. In my second-story bedroom, I hear footsteps climbing stairs, feel the friction of my father's hand skimming the rail, smell his bay rum wafting closer, listen to the dark power of his urgency nearing the door to my room, passing my sister's room . . . always passing my mother's deaf heart . . .

. . . walking closer to me. His breathing is loud and frantic. He strips off the sheet—no—it's the skin off my body—this body without protection. He whispers, "I love you so much," while he does *this* to my body. But what is *this*? Is *this* love? Is love a father who disrupts sleep and logic, who keeps me awake through wide hours of night, a man who leaves my room at dawn, not turning to see the wreckage?

I love you so much. Earlier, I erased that fiction writer's name from my Workbook, but these words he said to me remain embedded. At first I preferred to believe him— believe that he *was* the seemingly loving man adored by colleagues. Just as I wanted, as a child, to believe that my father, admired for his professional success, was simply the good man he seemed in public. Yet I came to realize that these two men who claimed to love me the most, claimed to care for me in the deepest way, loved and cared for me the least.

I lie on my bed in the hospital. From down the hall I hear laughter, voices at the nurses' station. I try to block out sound. I concentrate on darkness. I wait for a vision to appear as if in a spotlight. I want a sign that someone, some*thing*, will save me. I want something grand.

What?

A cathedral. Stained-glass windows. Incense. Low voices chanting. A mantra. Soothing words to save me from my addict self—that slut who waits under boardwalks and offers seedy kisses.

It is after four in the morning when something wakes me. From outside my door I hear a shuffle, wheels creaking. Must be that woman with the Ensure rolling her pole down the hall. Where is she going in her layers of sweatshirts, that thin shivering body? Who is she, that woman who never speaks?

I feel cold. I switch on the reading light and pull on my sweatshirt. I go to the door left partially open all night. I almost call out to her. We're the only two women awake, and I don't even know her name. But I don't want to see tubes forcing nourishment down her nostrils. Her slowly disappearing back is a faint smudge before she turns into her bedroom. And I no longer hear the wheels creaking.

Now the unit is quiet. The streets outside are quiet. All of

Atlanta seems abandoned in this fathomless, endless night. I feel alone. Alone on a unit full of women. The only other time I was surrounded by women (girls, really) was when I lived in a college dorm. Except I didn't feel surrounded by girls then, either. For my attention was always drawn outside my bay window, to men disturbing the nights of Boston.

In my Workbook I flip to the page where I made notes for my First Step, about the man I met on the bridge. Scrawled in the margin is Jill's phone number.

I pick up the phone and press the numbers. A buzz of static. Then it rings. Once. Twice. If I get an answering machine, should I leave a message? *Jill, are you okay? Tell me you want to come back.* Three. I almost hang up when a man answers, his voice groggy. I thought Jill lived alone. I apologize for the late-night call and ask to speak to her. The man says I have the wrong number and slams down the phone.

Of course she gave me the wrong number. Why hadn't I known?

I cross the room and sit at Jill's desk. I pick up the photographs and cards she ripped off the wall. One, the edges tattered and yellowed, is of a little girl in pigtails. She wears a Brownie uniform. Freckles, like Jill's, splatter her cheekbones and nose. She is grinning. One of her front teeth is missing. A wedge of a shadow, perhaps that of the person taking the picture, falls across her thin, bare knees. I turn the picture over. The name *Jesse* is printed in red ink. Jill's sister?

All of us thin-thin girls. Jesse. The woman with her Ensure. Me. My own sister, Kiki, two years older than I.

I think of a photograph of Kiki at Girl Scout camp when

we lived in the West Indies. In the picture she is so skinny, her image barely seems to adhere to the black and white print. She is surrounded by smiling scouts, yet her smile is the broadest, the most insistent, the most determined—so no one will notice her diminished body.

Kiki, I want to ask you, why are you afraid to be noticed?

I think of the Polaroid that Rick snapped in the Rainbow Motel. I wonder if, right this moment, he might be looking at it. The photograph. My body. But *it* is not *me*—although my body is part of me—the thinner, the better. Less body, less trouble. No body. *No* trouble. If no man is able to see my body, then I won't have to keep having sex.

DAY
THREE

AT SIX A.M. we line up for weigh-in. We stand on scales, backward, so only the nurse can determine whether those of us too skinny have gained weight, whether those of us too fat have lost it. We aren't allowed to know our weight because we're to stop obsessing about body fat, body image, what we look like, what we are eating.

After weigh-in we slip into sweats. For morning exercise we circle the hospital for twenty minutes. The first trace of light seeps across the cobalt sky. Yet warmth, light, seem far away.

Where am I going? Where do I want to go? Back to the Rainbow Motel to meet Rick? Or will I get in my blue

Honda and drive north up the parkway to Rome, Georgia, back to my husband, Andrew, to terrains of the ordinary and real?

Andrew, you will just be waking in your first-floor bedroom. After you turn off the alarm you will revel in silence, my noisy addictwoman gone from the house. Even though you know only a fraction of who I am and what I do, you must sense my whirlwind breath in the bedroom above you.

You know I am not well.

Summers, when the semester is over, you travel as far away from me as possible, to California to do research, or to Europe, chaperoning groups of college students on vacation.

I need you to chaperone *me*.

You won't. Of course you can't. Even if you wanted to, you couldn't. For my addiction is stronger than my love for you, even though I love you much more than this addiction.

You feel constricted and confused by my mood swings. This is why you will wake this morning and revel in silence. I see you sitting at the kitchen table, a blue bowl of granola before you. You will watch sports news on ESPN if the Braves won their baseball game the night before. If they lost you will watch CNN, not wanting to hear bad news.

You will do your best not to think about me.

If *I* were home now, I would be lying upstairs in my bedroom, but not sleeping. I would be waiting for you to leave the house. I know your routine—shower, shave, breakfast, dress for work—a routine that takes approximately an hour and a half. I don't venture from bed until I hear the front door bang shut, the car door slam, the engine of the car start.

It is only safe to slip from bed once you are gone. For this is when I begin my other life.

Men?

Writing about men.

Writers are told to write what they know.

There is only one thing I know.

Ted had told me to write in my Workbook about the men in order to expel them. Yet I've written about them for years in order to *absorb* them. It's the only way they won't abandon me. I create them with indelible ink—with the indelibility of words.

So when I'm not with a man I write a man, using addictive language of extreme connotation. As in life, I subvert definitions and am the ultimate unreliable narrator. Since to my addict, for example, the word *risk* means "normal living," *sex* means "love," *intensity* is "intimacy," true meanings dissipate until the reality of the object itself disappears. In the language of addiction, reality is ravaged by gothic nights dark with storm. Language is arcane. Melodramatic. This is the vocabulary I use in order to translate men into danger, the only vocabulary I know.

So how can I write when Andrew is home? My writing room, my head, are filled with secrets and men, and he'd feel them disturbing his tranquillity. He'd hear the ring of the obscene phone caller. He'd notice a mysterious scent of Eau Sauvage.

Only in isolation, after Andrew leaves the house, is it safe to travel in imaginary space to men's rooms, to incense and candles, to glasses of scotch, to wrinkled sheets, to bodies of no satisfaction. There is never enough satisfaction. So when I'm not with a man, I write a man . . . and need never be alone.

How else could I fill long weeks between Thursdays and Rick? Between Mondays, Wednesdays, Fridays, and . . . you.

I fill it with you. By writing about you, Man. I write in order to lust after fantasies of my own creation.

Except I don't write on Thursdays. I don't write when I meet Rick at the Rainbow Motel. The lure of a real seduction overwhelms all other words in any other vocabulary.

Nor need I write when I explore the contents of the wooden lavender box where I keep the photograph of me by the boardwalk. Dead flowers, napkins from bars, a piece of thread from a paratrooper's beret, books full of fiction, letters from across the States, scraps of paper from all the men I've never really known, from all the men who've never known the real me.

When I worked on Capitol Hill I had sex with a senator. I was a college student, a summer intern, and met him when I mistakenly rode a senators-only elevator during a roll-call vote. I wore a miniskirt and leaned against the wall, my hands behind my back, inviting him to look at my image, my

LOVE
IS
HERE
EVERY
DAY♣

image.

He did.

We had sex after work in his office, sex on a navy blue leather couch. I stole a gold United States Senate pen from his desk and saved a paper napkin from the Embers where we once met for drinks.

During the day I read the *Congressional Record* and the *Washington Post*. I drafted letters to constituents for the senator for whom I worked, answered telephones, ate lunch in the cafeteria, flirted with other student interns—did all this—while I waited for the six o'clock scent of blue leather.

On vacation in Israel, I once hitchhiked north from Aqaba and had sex with a paratrooper in the back of a military truck crossing the desert. I desired the tilt of his head in his red beret. I touched the blade of his knife with which he had slit throats of the enemy. He had a scar above his eyebrow. Another one, from a bullet, puckered his thigh. The air smelled of sweat and diesel and vengeance. Sun pulsed on the roof of the truck. Heat from infinite deserts rose up through the floorboards. His body was lean, hard—both imperiled and destructive—I felt it, like abrasive sand, hot as metal, on my body.

After spending one weekend with that writer of fictions, a man far more dangerous than the paratrooper, I felt too stunned to get out of bed. For three months, one full summer, I lay in bed sweating, barely eating, barely speaking, as if my throat had been slit by his dangerous words—lies. For his seductive treachery was an offer to marry me—to love, honor, and cherish me—when motel sex was all he was after. Yet I saved his fictional books, hoping to discover, in his *writ-*

ten words, one image that could soothe the wrath and rage and destruction he felt toward me and toward other women.

The words failed, of course. The moment his words tumbled from the page, I tried holding them up to the light. In the glare of sunlight his words deliquesced. I could only read them by moonlight, when language casts a hypnotic shadow.

I save everything in the lavender box: the scent of blue leather, a thread from a red beret, furious words of a writer. I believe if I read a letter, smooth a finger across a signature, I will know these men with whom I've had sex. These fetishes graft men's images into my consciousness.

I also believe these objects, or even a man looking at my body, prove *I* am real, that I exist, that I am a whole person, a breathing body. I won't see these objects as postscripts, meaningless footnotes to a narrative of an unlived, addictive life.

For years I'd hoped addictive language could create an illusion of verisimilitude. Now I must understand that that kind of language is counterfeit, a poor facsimile of life.

So now, here in the hospital, I must learn to accept that room #213 in the Rainbow Motel is only a sleazy motel room and that men who make obscene phone calls are not dependable lovers.

DAY FOUR

BODY IMAGE GROUP

In the lounge, I lie on the floor on a large sheet of paper. Linda, my partner, kneels beside me, drawing my outline. I feel the movement of crayon trail up my right arm and shoulder, around the top of my head, down the other side, past my waist, knees, feet. After she finishes, I draw hers. Now we're to color in our forms and depict how we see ourselves, or how we want to look in recovery.

I stare at my blank form.

Linda, in gypsy clothes, is drawing a business suit on her outline. The woman with the Ensure sits by herself in the corner. She won't let anyone near her, won't let anyone draw her image. Just as well. Her outline would be as thin as the I.V. pole—the tubes an umbilical cord—to which she's tethered.

I want to do this right. I want to decorate my form in the perfect outfit. I want to draw the correct clothes to conjure me into the perfect sober woman. But I don't know how this ordinary woman should look.

I lean against the leg of a chair. I can't *really* see this hospital, or who I am in it. I don't understand these bland colors, this sameness, day after day. In this air-conditioned unit there is no change in weather. No dust. No stains in sinks. No mildew in grout around the shower. No spider webs dangling from light fixtures in the ceiling. No old seasons leaning against bedroom walls and seeping into mattresses to remind us of everything we're to discard and forget. Here the air is always new, blowing through ducts. No past to color our forms.

I don't know how to absorb this newness. If only *I* felt new. If only I could change the texture of my skin, the color of my hair, the shape of my nose, the size of my heart.

Nancy, the nurse who conducts the body image group, sits on the floor beside me holding a box of crayons.

"I know this shouldn't be that hard," I say.

"Can you see you don't want to wear the clothes you wore when you acted out?" she asks.

I think of all the skirts and lacy blouses I left on the hangers at home in my closet.

I look at Nancy in a crisp plaid shirt, sturdy slacks, no makeup. How can she possibly understand *me*?

"Well," she says, "what you're wearing now is okay." She nods at my khaki shorts and white T-shirt. "Though I think it'd help if you tie your shoes."

"I don't want to," I say.

"Then how about just drawing your shorts and shirt?" She holds out a tan and white crayon. "Just try it." She nods at me, hopeful.

I take the tan and white crayon, then also select a red one from the box. I begin by drawing a big crayoned heart in the chest cavity on the piece of paper.

SPIRITUALITY GROUP

We sit in the group room with pencil and paper. Ted is telling us that, as we expunge our addiction from our minds and bodies, we must replace it with love and spirituality. He explains that those men with whom we act out are danger-ous (even if they don't threaten us physically) because, with them, we lose our spirituality, our souls. They are dangerous because, with them, we risk losing everything: our homes, partners, health, safety, our true selves . . . all hope we might have for love.

We must search for a Higher Power, whatever form we want it to take. I have read about this search in my butterfly-covered Workbook. I understand I must carefully follow, step by step, instructions listed in the book. I am to discover a route in order to journey through six long syllables of *spir-it-u-al-i-ty* and the slow, deep vowels of *soul.*

Except I don't know how.

Ted is right: it is those two solid syllables of *dan-ger* that block my passage. Danger. One word. Two syllables. Yet so many ways to define the word, too many definitions. Danger means murderers, rapists, child molesters, yes, but danger is also two emotionally dead people in a motel room at noon. Danger is Jill giving me a wrong phone number—and me wanting to call her. Danger is a man like that writer of fictions, offering love and marriage, when he really only utters these words as an enticement to fuck. Danger is husbands who don't see wives slip from homes to meet lovers—and wives who don't see husbands at bars with girls—what we all are capable of doing when we change our image to addict.

Today, Ted asks us to open our Workbooks to the page where we're asked to write a letter to our Higher Power.

I don't know what it is, what it looks like, how it sounds. How can I find spirituality with dreams of Rick in my head? Especially, how can I find a Higher Power here on this unit? If only this unit were more sacred, contemplative: no men dressed in black with white feathers, no women and bags of Ensure, no women in bangles and masks.

> *Dear Higher Power,* I write.
> *If only I were secluded in a convent. If only a priest with an aspergillum sprinkled holy water to cleanse stains that darken hearts. If only nuns cloaked my body in comforting*

*habits, soothing rage. If only angels expelled addictions with
wing-fluttering chants. If only I could bow my head at an altar
and be anointed "sober." If only my sins could be absolved
with an ash cross on my forehead, a wafer on my tongue. If
only I could follow drops of wax from white tapers down a
dark passage, through a black night. If only I could see flame
into the pure core of its light . . . then, maybe, I could find you.*

If only . . .

Danger is also here in my hospital bedroom. Late at night, I
wake to Gabriel's palm, firm on my stomach. I should be
startled. Or at least surprised. I'm not. These men are always
expected. Gabriel's tobacco-colored skin is sweaty, the scent
of fragrant obliteration. As he holds me without speaking, I
feel the denseness of his solitude against my spine. Blood
courses through my veins to flood the backs of my eyes. I
can barely see. My breath tastes like ether. If he stays much
longer I will sink into the oblivion of my body, a comfort I
always want.

"I've only got a few minutes," he says. He moves his palm
to the base of my throat. I trail my hand across his scar. "You
know, when you were looking out your window—that first
time?" He leans closer, and the tip of his braid brushes my
cheek. "You were looking for me."

Looking for him . . . but his reflection in the darkened
window a filter over my cornea, even before I met him,
obscuring perception. "Yes," I whisper.

"I wanted you, too," he says.

"You didn't—don't—know me," I say, half kidding.

"I imagine you," he says, not kidding. "And I imagine you don't much want to be here."

"I don't," I say. "But with you—"

"I want to meet you," he says. "Before supper tomorrow. Outside." He'll take me to a place not far from here in his pickup. "I'll bring a blanket. A bottle of wine. You'll have almost an hour before anyone'll notice you missing."

An hour.

I want a day. I want a night. I want a life. I want, at least, a month.

"It'll be beautiful," he adds. He presses his palm harder. This is what I must feel. This is what I must hear. This is what I must know. The real addiction? Not sex. Not food. Not alcohol. Rather, beautiful danger.

Yet when he clasps my shoulder, I feel the cold seed in the center of heat—that slow, silent numbing. As much as I want to believe him, want to spend my life, a life, with him, I also want to say, *No, I can't meet you.* I want to say to him: *Go.*

At that moment, I almost think I want to call to my husband to come for me, to save me. But to my husband, I am dim, hazy, unfocused. He doesn't hear me.

So yes, I say to Gabriel. I will meet you.

DAY FIVE

I STAND UNDER A RAINTREE by the curb of the hospital. I watch for the silver glint of Gabriel's pickup in the lowering sun. The air smells vacant with dusk. I can fill it with anything. I can fill it with you, Gabriel—touching the skin on my shoulder. Since I didn't bring my addict-clothes to the hospital, just before leaving my room I split the seam of my STRANDED ON THE STRAND T-shirt to expose my shoulder.

I sit on the curb. My untied laces look like pieces of trash. I haven't been outside at this hour since coming to the hospital. Nights are cooler. I imagine that next time I meet Rick at the Rainbow Motel we won't need air-conditioning. The swimming pool will be empty. The smell of chlorine will drain from the air. For twenty-four hours after I leave there, I always smell it in my hair. Now, I think, next time I meet Rick I'll smell particles of burning dust from the heater. Yes, I still have Rick and the Rainbow Motel . . . if Gabriel doesn't show up.

The traffic hum is distant, as if no silver truck will ever near me. The rising moon tangles in the top branches of rain-trees and pines, unable to shake loose and continue on a smooth journey. In the morning, I know, the sun will be too gummy and sullen to shine.

I wrap my fingers around my arms and shiver. Soon it'll be too cool to wear T-shirts at night, and I imagine mine on a clothesline all winter. Frigid. Rough. Wrinkles frozen in place. All winter the air from my lungs will taste like smoke and sulfur and rust.

I want to dissolve myself from this place. I can do this. If Gabriel doesn't come for me, my mind will travel to him— will cross the parking lot, the street, float down highways and across the universe . . . to hear him in faint vibrations from the moon, to taste him in moist veins of magnolia leaves as we journey straight to the heart of a destiny that always smells of desire and dusk. . . .

I imagine you, conjure you, into the kind of man who needs me. You're close to me, even closer, inside my head. Inside a trance . . . where I soothe myself with the pulse of my nighttime metabolism. In it, you will love me, desire me. You will soothe me through this night.

Slipping inside this trance, inside the addiction, is like slipping into a sphere where reality, guided by suns and moons, stops, and another reality, over which I have total control, because it exists only in my mind, begins. It is a fifth dimension, a secret room I enter and rearrange as if it is real space. If I don't like one particular section of it, I knock down a wall and rip out a ceiling. I reconstruct reality. I renovate and create it. In this trance, using the superhuman strength of the addict "me," I'm carried far beyond structured boundaries of life, beyond parameters of denotative language, signs, symbols, removing myself from a space I don't want to be in—this parking lot—to another one, now, with Gabriel. . . .

In a foreign universe. The color of saffron. We meet in the Hotel Majestic. He lies in a room, waiting. I hear his heart beating, echoing down the hall. I feel it, disturbing and erratic, along the floorboards to the soles of my bare feet, up my legs to my stomach, higher, until it pounds my own heart.

I cross the threshold. He lies in bed. The window is open and a marquisette curtain flutters. I see his black hair, the turquoise earring, the scar. I imagine my garnet fingernail tracing the scar, soothing it. He pours a glass of green crème de menthe. It wets my lips. I push it aside—not needing it. He pulls back the sheet and I nod, yes, this. We must explode our bodies out windows to our own planets, rocketing high to dark dimensions, not drinking crème de menthe . . . rather he is alcohol, and still we're rising higher toward spheres, toward secret rooms, toward that particular drink, where hands, as they stroke, numb what is feared, anesthetize what is lonely, suffuse what is empty . . . a sweet narcotic rush flooding my senses . . . plummeting me to numbness, to nothing, a massive emotional hemorrhage I crave. I

*believe I must cross thresholds to find these men, will always
have to enter these rooms in order to feel love. In order to feel
alive.*

I hear a voice behind me. It is Ted leaving the hospital.
"Come inside," he says. "There's nothing for you out here."

He is right. All I feel—all that's out here—is the cool
cement curb beneath my legs.

He is right: there's nothing for me *out here* because all I
really need to enter the addiction are the fantasies and
desires inside my own head.

In many ways, I *must* know that my fantasy Gabriel is better than the real Gabriel. Surely, I'd *rather* meet him in the
Hotel Majestic of my dreams than in his real silver pickup.
Otherwise, right now he'd be dropping me off back at the
hospital. I'd have to hear the truck door slam behind me. I'd
have to watch him pull from the parking lot and drive away.

And I must also know that the fantasy Rick is better than
our assignation in the Rainbow Motel. With Rick tucked
securely in my head from Friday morning to Wednesday
evening, I go to the drugstore searching for the perfect shade
of nail polish—heart-stopping red, silvery starlight, glittery
plum—which will make him love me forever. From Friday to
Wednesday I plan whether to wear red silk underwear or
lacy lavender. I try each on before the mirror in my bedroom
and examine my body. I buy new shampoos, lotions, soaps.
One of these, I convince myself, will make him crave me. In
this mental isolation in which I live, I can ignore everything

unless it has to do with Rick: my obsession. I don't want to know I use fantasy to distract me from real life.

By Tuesday of each week, Rick calls once a day. By Wednesday he is calling twice, whispering into the phone what he wants to do to my body on Thursday. *This* is the time I feel most strong and powerful—when I know he once again needs me—even though the power isn't mine, but belongs to my addictwoman. On Wednesdays, in my fantasy, I'm too high to remember that when he drives away from me on Thursdays, he never looks back.

Fantasies are more faithful, keep me faithful company.

Except here I am, alone on a curb outside the hospital. No man, no fantasy, no desire, no high.

There's nothing for you out here.

I ride the elevator back up to the sixth floor and go to the lobby across from the unit. The room is deserted, lit only by a small bulb attached to an aquarium atop a coffee table. I sit on the couch. Gold and black fish dart back and forth, up and down—trapped inside glass—nowhere to go.

DAY
SIX

I AM ALONE WITH TED in the group room for an individual therapy session. I slouch sideways on a wing chair, my legs over the armrest. Ted sits across from me, waiting for me to speak. The door and windows are shut. I think about not speaking, just listening to silence. To nothing. Though I don't meet his gaze, I feel Ted watching me, waiting. It's not that I don't want to talk to him; it's just that I don't want to talk at all, to anyone. There's nothing to say. Jill's gone. Last night, *I* could have been gone. No one can stop us. An addict wants what she wants when she wants it. An addict's favorite word is *now*. Her least favorite word is *no* or *wait: I want to leave now. I want a drink now. I want to die now. I want to fuck now.*

I refuse to wait. If this place isn't powerful enough to hold on to us, why bother speaking?

Ted puts the cap back on his pen and watches me with his steady eyes. "What're you thinking about?" he asks.

I shrug. "Nothing."

His smile is small. "If you did know, what would it be?"

This room with its pink and gray couches and easy chairs looks ordinary, yes, but now I wonder if we're supposed to pretend this *is* like a living room, a home, and we—all the women on the unit—are a family. Or at least we're supposed to figure out *how* to be an ordinary family. I rest my head back and stare up at the ceiling. "Jill."

"You miss her?"

"I guess. But I don't know why."

Maybe she reminds me of who I am *out there*. She's not a true sister. She's my addict sister. That's why I want her to get better. Because if *she* can't get better, how can I?

"What about you? What were you doing last night? You thinking of leaving, too?" I shake my head. He writes a brief note. I suspect he writes that I'm lying. When he finishes he nods toward the window. "*That* isn't where you'll find what you're looking for," he says.

Where will I find it? I wonder. Here? "Maybe," I say, "I wish I could just kind of live with you. For a little while. Then I'd be with a safe man."

"Except then I'd become like all those other men to you," he says. "There're other ways to feel close when you're lonely."

"Like how?"

"Like talking, the way we are right here."

His gaze is direct, gentle, unflinching. He does not stare at my body. He doesn't look away when I speak. Now, for the first time, I realize Ted doesn't look at me the way other men do. Rather, his gaze seems to dissolve that addict mask until I almost believe he sees a woman no one else has ever glimpsed, a woman I barely know myself. He sees *me*. I want to ask him what I look like, but I'm afraid to know.

"And by being honest and open," he adds. "With me and the women, your friends here. You know, if you'd gone to talk to Linda last night, maybe you wouldn't have had to sit outside on the curb all by yourself."

Closeness. Honesty. Real friendship. I hear Ted's words and understand the dictionary definitions. But I don't know how to translate his words into a language that will teach me how to change my rigid beliefs, my addictive behaviors, my heart.

"And you need to keep working on your First Step in your Workbook," he adds. "After you left home to go to college, how did the addiction duplicate what happened in your family? You told me about that older man you first saw out that window."

That man who gave me the maroon scarf.

"With him—all the men—the *real* search has been for family. To make up for what happened to you in your own family." Ted tells me to write about the patterns, the relationships, the men. "Since you've never known what a loving family looks like, you keep duplicating your own."

Repeating patterns. Duplicating men. The way my father

loved me made me feel worthless. The way these men love me makes me feel worthless, too. Yet I always believed if I didn't have *this* kind of love, I would be *un*loved. I would have nothing.

I stand to go. My hand on the doorknob, I pause. "That woman with the tubes . . ." I motion as if I'm pushing a pole. Ted nods. "What's her name?"

"She made me promise I wouldn't reveal it." He pauses. "She's very frightened."

"But she's *dying*."

"I know."

"Can't you stop it?"

"I don't know," he says. "We're trying."

WORKBOOK—FIRST STEP FOR ADDICTS

For several weeks, at three o'clock, I watch the man, old enough to be my father, from the bay window of my college dorm in Boston. Waiting to see him, I sit at my desk tapping a pencil in time to music playing on the radio: "This Magic Moment." I pretend to read a history of Western civilization. I feel the weight of the book, the weight of Western civilization, heavy on my mind, unable to contemplate so many historic events, memorize so many dates and facts. I gaze at one sentence, the words a blur, my breath shallow, my body weightless, my thoughts serial, as I mentally replay, over and over, the scene about to occur until the actual scene barely needs to happen.

There he is, the maroon-scarf man.

All my energy ebbs out my fourth-floor window and across the intersection. He leaves his apartment building carrying a basketball, the scarf much too elegant for his blue sweats. For one brief (magical) moment, he glances at me. Even though we neither wave nor smile, even though by now I've determined he's married, this is all it takes for me to feel that this is an authentic date.

He crosses the street, barely checking for oncoming traffic: all cars *shall* stop for him. Walking directly below my window, he looks up again. I turn to the other side of the bay and watch his back, his slow swagger. He bounces the basketball, this golden ball thudding like a heartbeat. The maroon scarf is more vibrant than autumn. His silver hair is more sunstruck than aluminum flecks on the Charles River. His potent image deflects sun, autumn, water, weather. Scenery is diminished by his presence, seemingly erased by the warm friction of his body moving down the street.

The subsequent wait, from three o'clock to five o'clock, when he returns from his basketball game, is, like the hours leading up to three, a dull surface of time gilded, on either side, by him. I wait—in an abstraction of time, place, thought, memory—until, moments before five, the *thud-thud* finally rounds the corner. I hear him before I actually see him, sound evolving as he approaches—closer, closer—into a force compelling enough to refocus my senses. The plangent thuds echo off Back Bay brick, causing small tremors in the center of my heart. I believe he bounces the ball as a signal to me, to alert me to his presence. It is a

secret code telling me he thinks of me. When he passes
below my window, I notice a patch of sweat under the neck
of his sweatshirt. He cuts across the intersection and bounds
up the steps, in black high-top sneakers, to the entrance of
his building.

I don't want him to disappear inside. I want to ask him
which apartment is his. I want to touch the shirts in his
closet, sit on the couch in his living room, taste the wine he
drinks for dinner. I want to know where he sleeps. Later
tonight, when the girls in the dorm are sleeping, I will slip
from bed to watch his building. A few scattered lights will be
shining. Are you there? Are you there? Or behind that dark
window, there? I will listen, trying to hear the *thud-thud*, the
urgent pulse of his dreams.

Now, as the door to the entrance slams behind him, my
breath feels truncated. My lungs are airless, sinking, flat.

I wait for tomorrow. I wait for three o'clock tomorrow.

I also wait for another three o'clock when I will not be
here at this window watching him, when I will be down
there with him, down on the street.

I flip to the index in my history book to search for the
word *sex*. No listing. I search for the word *affair*. Affairs of
state? All I want to know about these men who created
Western civilization is how they spent nights when they
weren't waging war, signing treaties, making pacts.

One afternoon, about five minutes after he returns from his
basketball game, a light comes on in a fifth-floor window.
There he is—the maroon scarf loose over his shoulders—

framed in the window watching me, framed in mine. The
room must be a library or study, and the bay just to the left
of this solitary window must be his living room.

He raises his arm. A wave? I pull my desk away from the
sill and press my palm to the windowpane. He mimics my
motion, a signal that he sees me. As if glass is permeable and
space illusion, I want to believe our palms touch. I open the
window and lean out. Wind off the Charles, damp and chilly,
blows my long auburn ponytail across my shoulders. The air
smells of autumn, a rich burgundy dusk I can almost taste. I
want to know his name. I want to inhale it. I want the breeze
to gust me across the street and into his life. He places his
other palm on the glass and bends his neck forward, nodding.

A woman moves next to him. I almost think I see a small
frown shudder her forehead, almost feel the torque of her
wrist tugging him from the window. No. Not yet. Wait. You
have him the rest of the night, spare me five more minutes.
Wait. I imagine her fingers, brittle with grief, will snap, leaving him to stray back to his glass sentry post: to me.

He pulls the shade. The light is turned off. Lights in the
bay window come on, gauzy behind a cloud of curtains. But
then night drapes are drawn across these day drapes. I can no
longer see in. He can no longer see out.

Who are you? Tell me who you are.

I know you will be in the bathroom washing up after the
basketball game, getting ready for dinner. You'll see your pale
face framed in the mirror . . . but I want you to imagine me,

my face, mine, lingering in the window. I want you to sense me in every shadowed doorway, every fold of curtain, every glimmer of light.

But he's washing up to eat dinner with her, his wife. I try to see through bricks, through walls, to the kitchen. She will be roasting a chicken. Wild rice boils and fresh vegetables steam. I wonder, even with such warm, nourishing food, whether they sit at a stark kitchen table—night closing in on them—eating in chilly silence.

Up and down the street, lights shine in apartments. Points of the sickle moon pierce the skin of the sky, spilling a fluid ocean of ink across the universe, filling the Charles River. Trees are silhouetted against brick. Leaves swirl down the street, gusting as if they've lost their way, searching for the ground. I want to find you, be with you—man with the maroon scarf—as much as I must believe you need me, too, need me to ease you through evenings of cool dissatisfaction.

The next morning, still in flannel pajamas, I sit on the corner of my desk. The shade in the study is raised again. There he is, at a desk, speaking into a blue telephone. I will him to notice me. I must sit here, wait here, until he does. I skip breakfast. I skip my first class. Finally, at ten o'clock, just as he hangs up the phone for the third time, he turns and looks straight at me. Milky morning light pours across his face. The glass on his window is refulgent in rays of sun. He seems to be wearing just a white undershirt, no long-sleeved shirt or sweater. His bare arms look cool, needy, ready. The distance of sidewalk and street, the thickness of glass, all evanesce. A

tincture of warmth touches my heart and my hands—deep
enough to warm him. I feel, in this one glance, I have known
him a long, long time.

Every few days I notice he parks a Mercedes in front of his
apartment building in a no-parking zone. He leaves the
engine running. I feel its faint vibration against the pane. He
loads a leather suitcase and briefcase into the trunk. His wife
stands beside him. She is thin, her cropped brown hair raked
back from her forehead with a hair band. When he bends to
kiss her good-bye, his mouth doesn't linger.

I watch the Mercedes disappear down the street, either in
the direction of Logan Airport or toward the interstates,
heading out of town.

His wife stands on the sidewalk and watches the car drive
away, too. I think I should wave to her, reassure her: he will
be back, he must come back to us. I could rush downstairs
and across the street and stay with her while he's gone. She
would fix me a cup of chamomile tea. Now we would be the
two people to eat dinner together in a cool, dry kitchen. I
wash dishes. Later, we sit beside each other in the bay window, silently watching for him to come back.

Now she turns and walks up the steps to her building. Her
legs, below her dark wool coat, are thin. There is an
exhausted slump to her shoulders, a weight to her back, as if
she's tired of waiting for this man and has been waiting for
him to return to her for a long time. I think I must hear her
sigh as the door whispers shut behind her. Tonight, I know,
her sighs, in her empty bedroom, will be deeper than the

city's rumble of midnight traffic, more sorrowful than bluesy music from bars in Cambridge.

Back then, I always wondered if my mother still sighed—weak and weary wives who lose husbands to young-young girls. Maybe after I left home it was my father who sighed. I always wondered how he managed without me, the daughter he made into his lover. Now that I am gone, I wonder where he sleeps, how he sleeps, without my warm, obedient body, without my heart beating in his veins.

For a few days, after the maroon-scarf man drives away in his Mercedes, he does not appear at three o'clock. I watch the doorway where he should be, imagine him on the sidewalk, the *thud-thud* sound. I miss him. No, I miss me. For only when he notices me am I able to identify myself: I am a face in the window.

One afternoon in November, promptly at three, I stand on the sidewalk below my window. First he glances up. No face. Slowly his gaze travels down the flights, down to me.

Bouncing the basketball, he crosses the street. When he reaches me he holds the ball in one hand up by his shoulder. It looks like a small sun, as if the sun has set early today, slipped from the sky, and landed in his palm. Then, I wanted to believe he was strong enough to hold the sun. I wanted to believe he was strong enough to hold me, a girl always on the verge of faltering—a girl accustomed to being held in the palm of a man's hand.

He's about a foot taller than me and bends his neck as he tells me his name. His smile is easy, his eyes gray and direct, his hair neatly clipped. His shoulders are broad and relaxed, comfortable on his frame. Older, yes, but he reminds me of Pat Boone or Troy Donahue with their airy, placid expressions, seamless faces light and bland, a reassuring constant, perfect for projection: this man *will* always want me, *will* always look for me at three o'clock, *must* always be who I need him to be. He has no dark secrets to wrinkle or worry his skin—I convince myself—relieved he looks like no one who could belong to my family. I like his last name, Forrest, better than his first name. This misspelled noun is what I will always call him.

"I wondered when you'd come outside," he says.

"Yes." I can think of nothing else to say in the presence of this man powerful enough to hold up the sun. I am a teenager without distinction or achievement. I feel silly, stupid, clumsy, awkward, weak. Here on the sidewalk, in public, all he'll see is a worthless schoolgirl; how can he want me or hear me? I step closer. The hem of my miniskirt barely trembles against a fold in his blue sweats. He must notice this, hear this, this rub of material, an urgent accent that tells him who I really am, tells him what kind of girl I can be with him—the only language I know he wants to hear, that I know he wants me to speak.

"You must like Frank Sinatra," he says.

Frank Sinatra? I like the Beatles, the Rolling Stones. "Yes," I say. "I love him."

"I knew it," he says. "You looked lonely up there in your window. Lonely people like Sinatra."

I think of Roy Orbison's "Only the Lonely."

"You look like you need a friend," he adds.

"Yes," I say. "I do." I need you.

"You know where the Ritz-Carlton is?"

I nod, figuring I can look up the address in the phone book. He glances at his watch. "I'm free tonight. You like Manhattans?"

"My parents live just outside . . ." I glance down, flushing. "Oh, yeah. Manhattans. Sure."

"The bartender at the Ritz makes the best ones in Boston."

He walks away, bouncing the basketball. He tosses it in the air with his left hand and catches it in his right. He juggles the sun, cataracts of light cascading over his body. I want to be cast in its blinding brilliance, want it to lighten this sense that I am too small, too hunched, too dark, too lost under the weight of secrets and shame.

Forrest and I sip Manhattans in the bar in the Ritz-Carlton. He wears a tweed jacket with the maroon cashmere scarf draped over his shoulders. The flame of a white candle wavers as he speaks. It is hypnotic. Just like his voice. My mind fades. *I* seem to fade . . . as if the Manhattan is elixir, his words secret potions to conjure this plain college student in penny loafers, knee socks, crew-neck sweater, miniskirt into a film noir image, the only kind of girl he could ever notice or need. I don't want to know that his words are merely tracks to a too-familiar destination—to a secret room I always enter, with a dangerous man I always crave but think I love.

The elevator glides us up to this room in the Ritz-Carlton.

We cross the plush carpet and gaze out the window—now, together—overlooking the Common and lights of downtown. His whispers tell me what he wants, what he wants to do to my body, to a body I believe he must fantasize in black silk. In a small gust of breath a black veil, attached to a velvet hat, trembles just below my eyes. He will lift the veil. My auburn hair isn't really pulled in a ponytail. Rather, it is swept into a French twist fastened with a diamond clasp. I imagine he unfastens it. I pretend my underclothes are lace, not cotton and white. Our mouths taste of rye, vermouth, maraschino cherry. I hear the sound of rustling sheets.

In his Mercedes, we drive back toward my dorm. "Wouldn't you rather have a real boyfriend?" He reaches over and puts a hand on my knee. "Someone you could spend the holidays with?" His grasp tightens. "I worry you'll be lonely."

We stop at a traffic light by Copley Square. "I'd rather have you," I say.

"I've been thinking," he says. "How would you like to work for me?" The light turns green, he puts the car in first gear, and we continue on. "Then, if my wife sees us together, she won't be suspicious." He tells me he usually has college students help him in his office located in his apartment. "You could come Friday afternoons."

I'm pleased he wants to see me again, that he wants me to help him, that I'll spend time at his apartment, almost as if I live there.

He stops in front of my dorm, the engine running. "You know how you could pay me?" I say.

I tug one end of his scarf, pulling it off. He laughs, not understanding, assuming I mean that sex would be payment. "No, just your scarf," I say. "That way I won't be lonely when we aren't together."

"Now, *that* would make my wife suspicious. She knows I always wear it."

"I'll buy you another one just like it. She'll never notice the difference."

He takes it and wraps it around my neck. He grips the edges, his knuckles against my collarbone. I clasp his hands, rubbing my finger across his slightly damaged left thumbnail, a small ridge down the middle, like a scar. "Give me one for Christmas," he says. "I got it at Brooks Brothers."

Back upstairs I watch his silhouette behind the curtain. His shadowy figure seems to glide behind a scrim. I watch until his wife shuts the thick night drapes that separate her husband and me. But doesn't she know we're only separated until morning, when her husband reopens them? Doesn't she know he will always want to see me here—every morning, every afternoon, every night?

Later, lying in bed, I press the scarf against my nose and mouth. I take a deep breath. The scent is of him—leaves smoldering in autumn dusk—and I believe it is a scent I have always craved, one I will always want. The tip of my finger still senses the ridge on his thumbnail. I don't understand why the scent of the scarf, why the ridge on his nail, seem more knowable, more definite, more tangible than the rest of him.

———

For my first day of work, Forrest sets up a card table in the living room just outside the door to his office. On it is a portable Hermes typewriter. He is a self-employed political activist. I am typing letters to organizations and universities around the country soliciting invitations for speaking engagements for him. I do not compose the letter, merely copy a form. I am a good typist. My fingers seem to read the letters and words more than my mind. From Forrest's office, I hear him talking and laughing on the telephone. I wish I was the one to amuse him. Except for his voice and the clicking typewriter keys, the apartment is silent. Forrest's wife, Shirley, whom I met earlier, is shopping. To the left of the bay window, beside the couch, is a Christmas tree secured in a red metal holder. The tree is not yet decorated. Boxes of ornaments are stacked beside it.

Muted light seeps through the curtain and across the green velvet couch. The velvet matches the material of the night drapes, now pulled open to the sides of the window. Forrest hangs up the telephone. I will him to walk out of the office. Stand behind me here, where I sit, on a metal folding chair. I will his hands to hold my shoulders. I will him to lead me to that patch of light.

My fingers lose their concentration. I transpose the letter *t* with the letter *h* in the word *the*. I remove a piece of correction paper from the plastic package, hold it against the transposed letters, restrike the keys. I fix the word. I can barely see the mistake.

I finish the letter and bring it to Forrest for his signature. His back to me, he stares out the window toward my dorm.

"I'm here," I whisper. "Not over there." I place my hands on his shoulders. He swivels around in the chair and I curl up on his lap. "In the flesh."

"Or almost."

"I could be."

"I wish." Gently, he nudges me off his lap. "Shirley'll be home any minute."

I look out the window, curious to see the dorm from his office. A girl with long blond hair, on the seventh floor, seems to be staring at me. I lean closer to the glass. Quickly she pulls back, out of sight. I wonder whether Forrest had been watching her. Now he's reading the letter I typed. He trails his hand from my hip down the length of my skirt until he touches my bare knee. I lean against his shoulder. I trace the outline of his lips, his chin, the top button of his flannel shirt.

I unbutton it.

The key turns in the front door. He nods at me to move to the other side of his desk. He fixes his shirt. I want to tell him these precautions aren't necessary, that his wife won't come here to check on us. Doesn't he know that? Why doesn't he know that wives would rather not see what their husbands do with young girls? The front door closes behind her. The rustle of paper bags. The door to the coat closet opens, closes. Her footsteps tap down the corridor to the kitchen.

"She's getting ready for dinner," he says. "Scottie usually comes over Friday night." His son is a senior in college. "You'd like him. He's on the basketball team. He's a swell kid. Maybe I should introduce you."

I can't tell if he's joking. I am not offended. I convince myself it would be another way to spend more time here. I like the word *swell*. I can't remember ever using it in this context. It sounds like a word from a film noir. I would use the word *cool* to describe a swell boy. "We could double-date," I say.

The soft skin around his eyes crinkles as he smiles. "Have you had many boyfriends?"

"A couple," I say. "In high school. But we never had sex."

This is true. In high school I had sex with my father. I also had sex with boys, but boys who could never be called "boyfriend."

He raises his eyebrows, questioning. He knows that the first time in the Ritz-Carlton wasn't the first time I ever had sex, that he wasn't the first man. I shrug and look away. There are no words to tell him who I was before he met me, when I lived at home with my parents. I have no vocabulary to explain about the nights my father slept in my bedroom, in my bed. I think of the transposed letters I typed. I think of myself as a transposed girl—like a letter always in the wrong place, with the wrong man. A mistake. The men, too, seem transposed. No, more than transposed: interchangeable.

"So who was the first guy?" he says. His tone is light, flirty, teasing.

This is the only time I've ever been asked this question. I open my mouth to answer, then close it. I feel as if all the air in the room presses the top of my head, forcing me to look away from him. I stare at the shiny pennies in my loafers. "I don't remember," I lie.

"That many?" he says.

"Oh, yeah, sure." My mouth and eyes feel as if a porcelain glaze hardens the surface, masking my real mouth, my real eyes, muting the real answer, the real childhood, the real me.

"You're some girl," he says.

"Guess I'm swell, too." I walk out the door and return to the card table.

I roll a piece of paper into the typewriter. From down the corridor I smell roast beef cooking. I imagine her slicing apples for a pie. The scent of cinnamon and clove. I imagine three, no four, china plates, with a warm yellow floral pattern, placed around the table in the kitchen. I press my hands to my stomach, suddenly ravenous. I'm thin, don't eat much, but I think about eating rare roast beef. I could eat an entire apple pie. I imagine Forrest and his wife sitting across the table from me and Scottie. While we eat, Frank Sinatra records are playing.

No, the records do not play. We would not need to listen to Sinatra while we eat dinner together. We wouldn't have to, for we would be a real family. Real families are never lonely.

I look at the blank piece of paper in the typewriter. *You're some girl.* I type my name onto the paper. I stare at the name, then type it again. How can I explain who this "some girl" really is, when I'm not sure I, myself, know? I don't understand how I can have sex with Forrest, be a film noir girl with Forrest, while pretending to be an ordinary college girl in front of his wife. I don't know how I had sex with my father while pretending to be an ordinary daughter in front of my father's wife.

I take out the paper. I rip the letters of my name one by one.

I cross the living room and walk, softly, down the long corridor, passing the bedrooms. I pause in the doorway of the kitchen. Her back is to me. She stands at the sink rinsing a mixing bowl. In fact, she is baking a chocolate cake. Not an apple pie. Three plates, not four, small roses rimming the border, are set on red place mats with matching napkins. A small crystal vase with a rosebud.

She senses my presence. She turns and smiles straight at me. I grip the doorjamb, almost misinterpreting the smile, transposing *it*. But the expression is not a frown, of course. For she doesn't know what I do with her husband. I return the smile.

She looks older than Forrest, her face more exhausted, her eyelids creased. Her hair is held from her face with a tortoiseshell band. She wears a plain black skirt and white oxford shirt, rolled to the elbows. Her legs don't so much taper into black pumps as stick into them, her calves barely delineated.

"Can I get something for you?" she asks. "A glass of water? A cup of tea?"

She thinks I have come here for water. She thinks I have come here for tea. Slowly I shake my head. Yet for a moment I almost forget why, this afternoon, I crossed the street, rode up in the birdcage elevator, opened the front door, entered the foyer, and, now, why I have walked down this corridor to this warm kitchen. For more than water, I think. For more than tea. For dinner? For food? To eat? To sit at that table with the pretty plates and rosebud? I want to ask her for something. I don't know how to explain what I want.

"No. Thanks," I say. "I was just leaving."

"Oh," she says. "'Bye, now. Have a nice weekend."

In the coat closet, her black wool coat hangs next to my brown suede jacket, the hood trimmed with fake white fur. There is an air of mourning about her coat and I smooth my fingers down the sleeve. One of the buttons is loose. Stitching is ripped from the collar, which is sagging. I feel so sorry for this coat. I want to tell it—I want to tell her, Shirley, I'm not trying to steal your husband from you. I don't know why I meet him at the Ritz. I'm not sure why any of this happens, why it seems as if it must happen. I can't stop it. I don't want to stop . . . as much as I don't want to remove my suede jacket from the hanger and walk out the door.

The following Friday a reel-to-reel tape recording of a Frank Sinatra concert plays. "The Lady Is a Tramp." Forrest zips his corduroy trousers. He fluffs the pillows on the couch and runs his fingers through his hair. I put on my underwear and pick up my red velvet ribbon that had slid onto the rug. Before I came over this afternoon, I tied this new ribbon that matches my miniskirt (as well as Shirley's kitchen place mats) around my ponytail.

"Time to get back to work," Forrest says.

"I love you," I say.

"Love you, too, kid," he says. "This is great having you here."

After he returns to his office, I continue to stand by the bay window next to the Christmas tree. It is now decorated with red and silver metallic balls, strands of tinsel, garlands of lights. Across the street, in my dorm, that window on the seventh floor is lit. I think I see the girl with long blond hair moving about her room. The window in my room is dark. Again, I think of the word *transpose*. If I were transposed to another window over there in the dorm, would I be a different girl, a different face in a different window? Maybe a college girl who studies hard, goes to plays and museums, a girl who understands why she's in college.

I hear Forrest talking on the phone in his office. I turn from the window and walk down the corridor toward the bathroom. I place my feet quietly on the wood floor as if I'm an intruder, a burglar. Forrest's voice fades. The reel-to-reel tape has ended. The air seems still, dustless, timeless. I pause by the partially open door of his bedroom. I nudge it wider. The air smells slightly of talcum, dry and insufficient. A smooth white bedspread. Crisp bolster pillows. I wonder how Shirley smooths out wrinkles in sheets and blankets and covers rumpled from Forrest's dreams, dreams that surely wrinkle the night, dreams and nights disturbed by my presence, so close to him, just across the street.

On the bureau is a photograph, maybe a wedding picture. Shirley wears a white tailored suit that reveals nothing of the form of her body, and a small white hat. Her smile is not flirtatious or coy or seductive. It is hopeful, I think, as she stares straight ahead toward the future. Forrest wears a suit that seems too large, maybe borrowed from an older brother. He

wears a hat like the kind in 1940s gangster movies, but his
placid smile is, even back then, pure Troy Donahue.

I look closer. Except, maybe I'm wrong. Maybe not Troy
Donahue. In a whorl of memory, I now think he looks much
more familiar to me than Troy Donahue.

The angle of the hat casts a shadow over one eye like a
patch. Shirley, gazing straight ahead with her hopeful smile,
does not look at him. Turn your head, Shirley, now, before
it's too late. Maybe you're not yet married. Turn now.
Quickly. Look. What do you see?

She does not turn. She does not see. My own mother did
not look before she married . . . did not turn her head to see
her pirate-husband, either. Or perhaps Shirley already knows
she can't prevent his pirate ship from sailing straight out of
their marriage, plowing perilous seas in search of me.

The air in Scottie's room is smoky and sleepy. The pillow,
on the knobby tan bedspread, is indented, as if he took a
long nap. There is a vague scent of marijuana and sandalwood. A stub of incense, surrounded by ashes, is in a bronze
holder. A stack of books: Hermann Hesse, Sartre, the *Bha-
gavad-gita*. On a lower shelf are albums by the Beatles,
Rolling Stones, Doors. I pick up a photograph of Scottie in a
basketball uniform.

In it, he seems too unsure to smile, a toughness under-
mined by pale cheeks that barely need shaving. He holds a
basketball like his father, but in this black and white photo
the ball is gray—not the sun. Instead, I think of his hands as
gentle enough to soothe a kid sister.

The guest room looks more like a girl's bedroom, a pink

spread on the bed. An antique vanity has a large oval mirror with a cushioned stool in front of it. I sit down and open a black-lacquered Chinese jewelry box with a mother-of-pearl design. Beside the box is an antique silver-plated hairbrush. Using this heirloom, I brush my hair up from my neck. Rather than fix it in a ponytail, I separate it into three equal clumps. Tightly, I braid the segments together and tie the ribbon on the end . . . so Forrest's autumn scent won't flow loose from my hair. So Shirley won't be able to smell it. A few strands of my hair remain caught in the soft bristles, the brush now seeming not so old, not so abandoned—or, as if everything in this room were now mine.

I have just returned to the card table when Shirley unlocks the front door, her arms full of shopping bags. She says hello and crosses the living room to the Christmas tree. Before removing her coat or scarf, she arranges packages wrapped in red and green and gold foil on the red felt tree liner. The boxes look as if they contain sweaters, shirts, ties, for the two men in her life. I haven't yet bought Forrest a new maroon scarf, but I will before I leave for Christmas vacation. Shirley rearranges the presents, stacks them this way and that, as if the perfect arrangement ensures perfect gifts, a perfect family, a perfect marriage, a perfect life. Her thin eyelids tremble. The bluish vein in her temple throbs. Listen, I want to say to her, what do you hear? Stop arranging shiny foil-wrapped boxes. What do you see? You see your family gathered around the tree Christmas morning, yes. You see Forrest on the couch opening presents. You see him here with his family. But how can you not also feel the weight of my brick dorm behind him, leaning against his back?

I begin to type again, picking up where I was interrupted when Forrest came out of his office and touched the nape of my neck. *Enclosed, please find a reprint of an article* . . . I watch Forrest's wife through partially lowered lashes. She hangs her coat in the closet. She unknots a blue chiffon scarf tied under her chin, a scarf that belongs to a different decade.

I stop typing. Perhaps it is the abruptness with which I stop that causes her to glance at me. I want to tell her to throw away the scarf, dab rosy color on her sallow cheeks and pale mouth. I want to warn her to keep the velvet curtains shut, during the day as well as at night. I want to tell her all this . . . as much as I want to drive away with Forrest in his Mercedes, my fingernails the color of garnets.

"Can I get you something?" she says.

My fingers, still on the keyboard, pause, as if about to type—not the rest of Forrest's letter—but something else *I want to tell you*, a secret message, my secret thoughts, a warning that can't be spoken. "Oh, no, thanks," I say. I can neither speak nor type this warning, as if all important words are illegible. "Just—your tree." I nod at it. "It's so pretty."

She walks forward and stands at the edge of the wood floor in the foyer next to the living room rug. "I love Christmas." She shakes her head. "Look at that. I forgot to plug in the tree."

"I can get that for you." I push back the chair.

"Maybe you'd like to stay for dinner," she says. "Scottie'll be over shortly."

Four plates with the rose pattern are arranged on the table in the kitchen. Tonight, instead of a rosebud, two red candles are placed in the middle of the table. Scottie, in bell-bottom jeans and a ripped sweater, with dark blond hair almost to his shoulders, sits across from me, Forrest and Shirley on the opposite sides. Two men, two girls, a balance and symmetry that, to me, must be a perfect family. In fact, I convince myself I have been invited to dinner because I complete this image. I imagine they will urge me to move out of my dorm. They will ask me to live here. I can type Forrest's correspondence. I can place my necklaces in the Chinese jewelry box. I can help Shirley cook dinner. I can be Scottie's sister. I can be Forrest's . . .

Carefully, I cut meat loaf into bite-sized pieces. I make sure each piece is secure on the fork before lifting it to my mouth. I clasp my water tumbler in a fist. I don't want to make a mess, do anything to draw attention to myself, worried, if I spill a drop of gravy on my yellow poor-boy sweater, Shirley will somehow see all the mistakes, all the messes, all the stains, all the hair in disarray, all the wrinkled and quickly discarded clothing, and will know what Forrest and I do together on her pretty green velvet couch when she is out buying Christmas presents.

I must appear perfect. Just like my family. At home, my important father sat at the head of the dinner table surrounded by his well-mannered wife and his two well-dressed

daughters. We ate perfectly prepared meals served on Wedgwood plates using sterling silverware, perfectly polished.
Shirley's silverware is shiny, too. I pick up my spoon and turn
it in my fingers, seeing this spoon, all the spoons in my
mother's kitchen, all the polished spoons that reflect a family's shiny, perfect surface.

Scottie turns to me. "How long you been working for
Pop?" His smile, like his father's, is easy, his front teeth
crooked, his blue eyes clear and studious behind wire-
rimmed glasses.

"Just a few weeks," I say.

"Don't let him work you too hard. His last secretary quit
in a huff."

Forrest never told me about a secretary. He never told me
about a huff.

"I'm not really a secretary. I'm just . . ."

"And don't let him make you go over to Belmont and spy
on the Birchers. They're a scary bunch."

"Oh, no, Forrest just wants me to . . ."

I stop speaking.

As I say the word *Forrest*, Shirley's hand, about to butter a
roll, pauses. Her lips compress, tightening. She does not swallow the piece of meat she just placed in her mouth. Vein-
webbed skin below her left eye spasms—this, the only
movement.

Even though *Forrest* is a formal last name, I should not call
him this in front of his family, I realize. For I do not use it
formally, of course.

I think I stop breathing. No one seems to be breathing, as

if the air drains from the room. Even the candle flames seem to sputter with lack of oxygen. As air seeps away from us, I imagine it infiltrating wooden chests where wives store silverware in blue velvet liners. The air will breathe against silver. Tarnish it. No more perfectly reflected surfaces.

I want to fix my mistake. I don't know how to fix it. I want to gently touch the skin below Shirley's eye in order to comfort the spasm. Now I think I should not have left strands of hair in the brush. I grip the napkin in my lap. I want to hide the hands that touch her husband. I want to hide everything.

But now Shirley is calmly spreading a dab of butter on the corner of a roll . . . almost as if the pause never happened. I glance at Forrest. He winks at me over the rim of his wineglass. Scottie flattens mashed potatoes with the back of his fork like a little kid and begins to talk about the Celtics.

Maybe no one really heard me. Maybe no one understood. Maybe everyone thought I said Mr. Forrest. Maybe I can still be a young college girl, as I appear to be. Yes, when we finish eating, I will dutifully offer to help Shirley wash dishes.

The flames on the candles once again flare with the force of breath. I think of the candles in the bar at the Ritz-Carlton. I don't understand why I am lured by that flame, there, as much as I am lured by the flame here in this kitchen.

I stand beside Shirley at the kitchen sink. She plunges her hands into dishwater. All her knuckles are swollen as if cramped with arthritis. She wears a diamond ring with a gold wedding band that would never slide off over those knuckles. She places dishes in a rack. I remove them and wipe each plate until it is bone dry. I am speaking, trying to tell her about my courses, my professors, convince her I am an ordinary student. But my voice sounds shrill, I know, and false. For I am not this student I am describing. I speak, hoping the patina of truth—that I am in college—this one thin dependable surface truth can gild the core of truth that isn't mentioned: that I am really a girl who spends all her time watching men out windows. In the dazzle of false words, I hope true words that might explain why I called her husband Forrest will not be required.

Now, from down the corridor, I hear Forrest and Scottie talking above the chatter of the television. Slowly, I wipe each piece of silverware until it is dry and spotless. I trail the dishcloth across each pot and pan, lingering. When Shirley and I finish in the kitchen, maybe we'll brew hot chocolate or a pot of tea. We'll join Forrest and Scottie in front of the television. The hour will grow late. We'll all be sleepy. Too late for me to return to the dorm. They'll invite me . . .

After she places the last plate in the rack, she shakes water off her hands and pulls a dry cloth from a drawer. "Well, I guess that's that."

She blows out the candles. I don't want her to leave the kitchen. I want her to stop. I want to sit at the kitchen table. I want her to sit beside me. I want to open a schoolbook. I want her to help me with homework. I want her . . .

"Finished?" she asks.

"I thought maybe I'd bring Mr. Forrest a cup of tea. And Scottie. Would you like tea?"

She looks at me one long moment. Her eyes narrow. Her

smile is chill and antiseptic. "You're such a sweet little girl," she says. "So helpful." She snaps off the light.

A concussion of shame explodes at the base of my skull. My feet seem mired in sludge as I follow Shirley down the corridor to the living room. Forrest has folded up the card table and put it away. Faint marks from the legs remain embedded in the carpet. Forrest and Scottie sit beside each other on the couch watching television. There is only one easy chair, on the other side of the Christmas tree, which, I know, is Shirley's. There is no chair for me. There are too many of us. While we seem to be only four people, we are not. We are a slur of fathers, lovers, boyfriends, sisters, mothers, daughters—and competition. So many people, but only enough chairs, only space enough, for three.

Shirley opens the coat closet and removes my coat. Forrest smiles and makes a small gesture, like a wave, and thanks me for typing his letters. Scottie says it's nice meeting me. I try to thank Shirley for dinner, but my voice is so dim I'm not sure I'm speaking. I feel something faint, like a scared moth wing, flutter against my heart. If only the sound were louder. If only someone could hear it. If only someone would ask me to stay in order to listen.

I take my jacket and jam my arms into the armholes. Out on the landing I wait for the birdcage elevator to clank up to the fifth-floor landing. I open the sliding gate and slam it behind me. The elevator rattles downward. I think I don't want it to stop. I want it to crash through the floor of the lobby. I want to tumble downward to other levels and layers of understanding, of misunderstandings, until I hit bedrock. Until I am a real girl standing on solid ground.

I am out on the front stoop. Snowflakes furl around street-lights before melting against the glass fixtures. Wind off the Charles blasts my cheeks and unprotected neck, since I can't wear the maroon scarf when Forrest's wife might see it. I don't zip my jacket. Across the street all the windows in the dorm are lit. To me, the lights aren't welcoming. I don't want to enter the dorm. I don't belong there. I am not a college student.

I back out into the middle of the street and look up at For-rest's windows. A car swishes past blaring its horn and sends slushy snow across my feet. A shadowy form stands beside the Christmas tree. She holds back the edge of the curtain. But don't you know: there is no reason for you to fear me. He'll never choose me. I don't know how to be a wife with a diamond ring, a wife with hands plunged into dishwater, a wife with swollen knuckles, knuckles swollen from hard work, the hard work of loving and raising a family. After all, how can I know how to be a wife if I have never known how to be a daughter?

I whisper her name. I want her to hear me. I want her to see the true-true me, a girl whose hair needs brushing, as if she could glean that image of me in the guest-room mirror and hold me. And help me.

The curtain slides back into place. I remain in the middle of the street watching the darkened window.

Still, I want to believe, I must believe, that invisible moons revolve to cast me into another orbit, into another family, *this* family—I want this family—that must be constellations away from my own.

Suppose I'm not cast into this family?

Suppose this family is not really all that different from my own?

I cross the Common holding a box from Brooks Brothers, in it an identical scarf. The old scarf warms my neck. My green bookbag is hitched over my shoulder. I hurry toward the Ritz-Carlton, toward the bar. Him. The snowy path is dark. Almost seven. I hear two sets of crunching footsteps just behind me. I slow to let them pass. They don't. I hurry again—not to escape the footsteps, walking at the same pace as my own, but because I'm anxious to see Forrest the last time before Christmas vacation. In the distance, church bells chime. A faint din of traffic rumbles down Arlington. Over by the pond I hear laughter. But all sounds—except the footsteps following on the path with tamped snow—seem muted, quickly fading, unable to resonate against a ground feathered with snow. A woman with a dog hurries past. Couples, bundled against the cold, hold mittened hands. I clutch the white box tied with a red ribbon more tightly as if to prove I am not alone. I am part of a couple, too, hurrying to deliver a Christmas present. I am also not alone because the two sets of footsteps still follow, an echo of my own, faint aftershocks that don't stop.

I am several yards from the hotel when the footsteps seem to stumble—no, they rush forward until one set of thick rubber boots is on my right and one is on my left. Two bodies, male bodies, in ski caps and dark parkas, press either side of my brown suede jacket, pinning my arms. I can't distinguish features or limbs, just feel a heavy, burly presence filling the sidewalk. Their boots kick small drifts of snow onto my loafers. The nylon scratch of parkas now obliterates the sound of footsteps, theirs and mine. The men smell of leaf mold and fireplace cinders—a drowsy hibernal scent that presses my brain and the backs of my eyes. We walk rapidly, in sync, but I no longer feel my legs beneath me.

When they finally speak, their voices are muffled. Their words seem to reach me through layers of parka and ice. I hear something like, "Hey, want to come with us, baby? . . . Come on with us. *Come on.*"

The last "Come on" sounds unexpectedly young and sharp and urgent. So I think maybe they're kidding, and a small, shrill laugh bursts from my throat. I shake my head, saying, "I'm busy. I'm going to meet my boyfriend."

They're closer still. Even in the cold I feel the heat of their bodies. "Hey, come on, *we* want to be your boyfriend."

They are not kidding.

They halt and turn facing me, blocking the sidewalk, just beyond light that spills from the windows of the Ritz-Carlton.

A knife.

It must have pressed my arm or my side, but I hadn't felt it. I glance at the man holding it. His eyes are watery. His lips are pale with winter. The tip of his nose is damp and raw. His hand gripping the knife trembles.

I almost feel sorry for him, for his paleness, for his nose

that needs wiping. I believe he trembles because he, too, is exhausted, having traveled here from a vast distance searching for me. I don't think he wants to hurt me—not really—but he doesn't know how else to get what he wants.

I clutch the box with the scarf tighter, worried it will be stolen. I could give him the shiny pennies in my loafers. Or my wallet. I hold out my bookbag, a small offering to appease his exhaustion and hunger. With the knife he swipes it away. I lose my grip, dropping the bookbag in the snow.

I understand I can't appease with money. I can only appease with me.

I reach into my coat pocket for a tissue, thinking to offer it to the man, thinking I should offer to wipe his nose.

My movement startles them. *They* step back, away from me. I almost laugh again.

My pockets are empty. I have no tissue.

I stare at the knife, confused. What do they want from me so badly they need a knife to get it? You don't need a knife, I almost say. Don't you know me? I already know you. I already taste your mouth scented with metal.

The man jabs the knife toward some distant point behind my back. "Come on, come on, get going."

"But my boyfriend . . ."

My first thought is that if I don't meet Forrest in the bar, he will be angry I broke the date. He'll never see me again.

Yet my second thought, one that's as thin as the blade of the knife and as painfully sharp, is that I am flattered, albeit uneasily, that, of all the girls in Boston, these men chose me.

I pause.

Why isn't Forrest here with his sunlight to find me?

I glance up at the windows of the hotel, half believing I am already upstairs with him and I will see myself, like a twin, gazing down.

Or it is Forrest I see in the window, beckoning, his gray eyes glinting like metal.

Some hotel windows are dark and hollow and empty. Others look as white as a blind eye.

Still I pause.

It is this pause that is crucial. It is this pause I must remember and respect, this pause inside which I must learn to stand, learn to stop, learn to wait. I must widen it, stretch it, until it is this soothing, circumambient pause itself in which I live, not the danger singeing its border.

Still.

Which man? You, Men? Forrest? Who needs my body more badly?

Inside my skin, I hear only silence. I don't know where I'm supposed to go, what I should do. I don't know whether to turn in the direction the man with the knife points or not.

A group of people—the doorman? I'm not sure, I can't tell, it happens quickly—leaves the entrance of the hotel. They see my bookbag in the snow. They see two men facing me. They see my body, still trapped in the pause. People shout and hurry toward me.

The men flee.

Someone asks what happened, what happened?

"Nothing," I say. "Nothing." This must be true.

Are you hurt?

No, no. It's nothing, I assure them, backing away.

I can't enter the hotel. In the light, these decorous people will see some mark on my face. I don't know the size or shape of it, only know it feels dark and heavy, like shame.

I grab my bookbag and walk around the block. I only remember a vague body turning corners. I only remember the pressure of fingers clutching the white box with the pretty red ribbon. I remember empty loafers crunching snow on the sidewalk. Wind whipping eyes that don't blink against winter. I don't remember *me*. I feel suspended between the girl I appear to be . . . and one who could never be that person—rather, a pale girl I must have lost somewhere. I don't look over my shoulder. I do not fear that steps follow.

Forrest sits at our table in the bar, two Manhattans placed on cocktail napkins. He asks why I'm late and I tell him stores were busy. "Christmas shoppers." I hand him the present. The ribbon is askew, but he doesn't notice. A cool breath lifts through my body and I shiver. He doesn't notice this, either. My smile is too blinding, too glassy, too insincere. I feel as if I have been unfaithful to this man who waited close to an hour for me in the bar in this expensive hotel. I tell him I was worried all the maroon scarves would be gone and I'd have to give his back.

He listens to me, nods. Yet he seems distracted, fiddling with the napkin. One edge is shredded into pieces. He drinks half the Manhattan and taps the glass down too hard. His wallet is on the table as if he were about to pay the bill and leave. His glance slides across the room to other tables. Other women. Maybe he grew bored waiting for me to arrive—or maybe just bored, period. I want to be witty, entertaining. I'm not. Even now, with Forrest, I am exhausted.

Tonight I don't drink the Manhattan. I bring the glass to my mouth just to wet my lips. I want to feel the sting of alcohol on numb lips, as if alcohol can be a stimulant that will jolt me awake. It isn't. Even in this drowsy state I must understand the problem: there is no reason for us to be here in the bar. Alcohol does not entice. He knows this, too. He drums his fingers on the table, waiting for me to finish the drink. Here, we have nothing to say to each other; there is only one place we can speak.

"I don't want it," I whisper. I slide the drink away from me. "Never mind."

Upstairs, he turns off the lamps. We lie on the bed. He touches me and I take a deep breath. My lungs brim with the scent of autumn-knives-ice, jarring me back to life. In the heat of Forrest's hands, my skin finally feels blistered awake. I whisper over and over that I love him. This *must* be love, for I don't know what else it could be.

Except now, when it is over, the exhaustion I felt in the bar deepens as I lie, unmoving, on white anemic sheets. I feel as if I'm in withdrawal with no opiate to prevent this painful dissipation. Lights from downtown cast shadows across our bodies. Even this seems too bright. My lids lower. Forrest blurs. His eyelids are blank as masks. Our bodies next to each other in bed seem so distant I can't remember why we're here, and I have a small dread I shouldn't be here. I have a small dread I should have fled the men with the knife . . . that I can still run, that time has not moved forward and I can still hide. I try to wake. To move. To leave. I can't. I feel as if I have swallowed the sky, lungs liquefied to vapor.

I focus on the picture of mallards hung on the wall across the room. They look like spirits, in flight.

Forrest turns and opens his eyes. He rubs my shoulder. His hand feels warm, but the touch is cool. Like freezer burn. But this intensity must mean he still loves me—must mean I'm all right.

Later, when we dress to leave, he lowers his undershirt over my own head. He wants me to sleep in it when I'm away over Christmas.

"I can't wait to see you after vacation," I say.

His face, not just his mouth, seems to hesitate before he speaks. "We might have to back off a little after the holidays. Shirley. I think she's suspicious."

"Back off?" I say.

"Just a little."

"I love you."

"I know. But maybe it'd be better if you don't work for me anymore. If you don't come over."

But I'd rather be over there than here, I think.

"My undershirt and scarf'll keep you nice and warm," he says.

But what happens to this nice warm body if he no longer needs it?

Back in the dorm, I rush upstairs and look out my window. Behind the curtain, I see muted green and red Christmas tree lights. His silhouette seems to face my dorm. Yes, he watches for the light in my room, so he can see my spectral image, too.

Yet I don't turn on my light. A thin figure sidles next to him. Shadows shift and fade. Yes, his wife is suspicious that his gaze, as well as his heart, has sailed away from their apartment, away from her, away from his home, here, across the street, to me. He *must* still want my body.

A few moments later the velvet drapes slide across their window. I know his wife closed them. She must have. Not him. But doesn't she know a filament of light still illuminates the edges?

I whisper his name.

The line of light is extinguished. They are over there, that family with a Christmas tree, getting ready for bed.

I press my hands to the windowpane. Ice blisters the glass. A winter moon watches me. I don't want to know the moon has no light of its own, only reflects light from the sun, its warmth now switched off for the night.

I slip under the covers wearing Forrest's scarf and undershirt. I can't sleep. The steam radiator hisses and gurgles. In the corridor a girl shuffles in slippers to the bathroom. In the adjoining room girls laugh. Out the window traffic murmurs along Beacon Street and Storrow Drive. To me, these ordi-

nary sounds seem foreign. These reassuring sounds that life
spins safely on its axis seem to reach me, always, from a distance. If only I could stay here in this room, sleep in this bed,
in this dorm, and let this comfort wash over me. Or, if I
could live in that apartment across the street, not alone with
Forrest, but with his son and wife, too, a daughter's solitary
bed with an innocent pink bedspread, in a daughter's solitary
bedroom—but one with a lock on the door, not like my bedroom door at home, rather, with a lock to which no man has
the key.

I go home to New Jersey for Christmas vacation. After a
shower one morning, I leave Forrest's undershirt in the bathroom by mistake. My mother throws it in the washing
machine with the other laundry. I wait for the clothes to
wash, to dry, then dump them on the kitchen table. I sort
through the pile, folding underwear, towels, sheets, socks. I
examine and fold each undershirt but I can't find Forrest's,
the same size and style as my father's. I try to distinguish a
texture or stitching that would differentiate his. They all
look the same: bleached snowy white.

My father comes in the kitchen and turns on the kettle.
Since I left home for college he no longer touches me. He is
a child molester; I am no longer a child. He stands by the
stove measuring coffee into a mug. One, two, three, four tea-
spoons of sugar—sugar, I believe, to numb whorls of desire
coursing through his body. We don't speak. He doesn't think
to ask me about classes or college or friends. He seems

almost surprised to see me here in the kitchen, as if he has only a vague memory of me, of what I used to be to him. We glance at each other coolly, strangers.

The kettle whistles. My father pours water into the mug. His features blur behind steam. I have never seen him more clearly. Floating behind my consciousness is a fear that I have grown up to be the daughter he raised, that he would be proud of me, his daughter who warms dangerous men on frigid nights, who entices men with wives whose eyes do not see what they see.

I pick up the stack of undershirts and press them to my face, hoping Forrest's will smell different. But they all smell the same.

In March, Scottie invites me to a coffeehouse in Cambridge. Even though Forrest and I still meet on occasion at the Ritz-Carlton, I know, in another sense, he is gone. Since I don't want to assess the limits or depths of the loss, I must accept Scottie's invitation. Otherwise, the missing of Forrest will froth up around me. The only way to quell it is to inscribe another man's image onto my consciousness.

How easily I recostume myself to match this new image. To match you, Scottie. Here in the coffeehouse, I am no longer Forrest's film noir fantasy. How easily I bifurcate into Scottie's hippie flower child in granny glasses and dangly earrings—in sync with his scraggly blond hair, sideburns, bell-bottoms, paisley shirt. I sip cinnamon-spice tea—no Manhattans here. The room is smoky-blue-viscous. A folksinger strums a guitar. Voices are low and earnest. We are serious about civil rights, Vietnam, the generation gap, the draft. No, *they*, restless college students, are serious. My own restlessness, my earnestness, are pretense.

We return to Forrest's apartment. Forrest and Shirley are out. Scottie brings me to his room. He opens a window and lights a stick of sandalwood incense as well as a joint. The Doors play on his record player—no Frank Sinatra tonight. I sit on the floor, my head against the wall. The beat throbs my skull. "Break On Through (To the Other Side)," "Twentieth-Century Fox," "Light My Fire," "Back Door Man," "End of the Night." The record turns. Songs slide together. Scottie offers me the joint. I shake my head. Grass isn't the drug I'm after.

But a slow swirling lassitude surrounds me. Still I sit on the floor, Scottie on a chair across the room. The distance between us seems interminable; tonight I am unable to seduce this drug I'm after. Percussive vibrations from the Doors are exhausting. Scottie's foot taps the floor, not in time to the music. He's zoning on grass, the smell enervating. Smoke from marijuana and incense puffs across the room before curling out the window. A thin gray haze skims the surface of my mind.

I should not be here, I think.

As Scottie takes a drag, the red ash on the end of the joint flares. I try to think of this as a warning. A small flare warning me. Of what? What kind of danger?

———

Forrest and his wife return. Voices. Footsteps down the corridor leading to their bedroom. They don't knock on Scottie's door. I don't know if Forrest knows I am here.

I am here. I am not here. I am at home in New Jersey sorting through undershirts. My father watches me through steam. Forrest watches me through blinding sunlight. What do they see? What do they want? Where are the mothers? They are not watching me. They see nothing.

I kneel before Scottie. I take the joint and place it in the ashtray on the floor. I rest my arms on his thighs and press my head against his chest. His heart beats slow, soft. I barely hear it, a low monotone—throb, throb, throb—over the music. I want it to beat louder. His weary mother; his distracted father: no one hears Scottie, either. I must hear him. I tug the tips of his collar. His eyelids flutter open. He removes his wire-rimmed glasses. His soft curtain of hair brushes my cheek. I feel a flutter in my chest. Yes, small pulses of love, a druggy haze of desire. It must be. I close my eyes and lean toward it, lean toward oblivion: all that I desire. Scottie kisses me. Now my mind swirls in a small confusion. His mouth tastes dry and sooty . . . and I'd almost hoped for rye, vermouth, maraschino cherry.

I roll back from him and sit flat on the floor.

"What?" he says. "Come here. *You're* a twentieth-century fox."

Or a lady who's a 1940s tramp.

I'm either. Or neither.

I walk down the corridor to the foyer. I open the coat

closet. Sliding my jacket from the hanger, I brush against a ski parka. The rustle reminds me of the men with the knife, their parkas. I trail my hand along other coats and jackets until I find Forrest's new scarf. In its newness, it just smells like material. He and his autumn are gone.

Faintly, from Forrest's bedroom, I hear "It Was a Very Good Year." From Scottie's room, the Doors sing "The End."

Does it matter which singer, which song? Does it matter which boy, which man?

Does it matter which bedroom door I open? Which singer I hear? Which man I fuck? Frank Sinatra? Jim Morrison? Forrest? Scottie?

Does it matter which girl I am?

All I want is to be an ordinary girl: one who is seen, one who is known, one who matters.

DAY
SEVEN

THURSDAY, FROM TEN A.M. TO ONE P.M., is visiting day. At a quarter to ten I go to the lounge to wait for Andrew. I sit on a chair by the window and glance outside into the drizzly day, searching for a gray Ford Escort station wagon, trying to will it into the parking lot. I have washed my hair and put on my best T-shirt to appear as normal as possible. I want him to see, if not full success in my recovery, at least potential. I want to promise Andrew, *I will get better, I will get better, I will get better.* I want to explain to him what I learned last night about myself from writing in my Workbook, and from Ted: that maybe all I ever wanted was a family.

In the lounge, serious parents talk with daughters. Serious

husbands talk with wives. Voices are hushed as if someone has died. Sheila sits alone in the corner knitting a mustard-colored sweater. Linda's husband, short and stocky with close-clipped brown hair, sits on the edge of his chair ready to bolt. He wears a three-piece suit that looks particularly formal next to Linda's flowing clothes. Her brown hair, streaked with gold, is neatly braided and coiled around her head. She is crying. Her husband makes no move to touch or reassure her. He stares across the room, his lips pressed together. She touches his knee. He pulls his leg back as if singed.

Andrew, I don't want to scare you.

Except I imagine a little-boy Andy, a boy who *should* be scared by the adults around him. Andrew, that little boy, grew up with a silent and distant father, frequently absent from home. Andrew didn't know why.

Andrew's father was employed in manufacturing. Once, when he was transferred to another state, he left his family behind for several months, claiming he needed to find them a new house by himself. During this time without her husband, Andrew's mother told Andrew, little-boy Andy, still in elementary school, that he was now the man of the house.

At first, perhaps because he felt lost without his father, Andrew was afraid to go to school. Only when he saw one of his friends walking home with a toy drum made from a Quaker Oatmeal carton did he return to school. He wanted a toy drum, too.

Late one night he discovered his mother crying over a heartbreak song she played over and over on the record

player. He tried to comfort her. But Andrew never understood—even though he was now the man of the house—
why he couldn't make her happy.

I can't make Andrew happy, either. I am like his straying
father. I am also like his mother, crying over heartbreak men.

At eleven-thirty I stand and stare out the window. Maybe
Andrew forgot which floor I'm on and is searching the hospital. I scan the rows of cars in the parking lot. I watch the
entrance to the hospital. Every time I catch a speck of gray,
my heart lurches. But no gray Ford Escort turns into the lot.

No silver pickups, either.

Outside, red, yellow, white umbrellas twirl in windy rain. I
press my palms and forehead to the windowpane. I want
someone to look up to the sixth floor and see me. I want
Andrew to see me.

He doesn't know how. He doesn't want to see me here in
the hospital.

My watch says noon. Today is Thursday. Every Thursday at
noon . . .

Rick. The Rainbow Motel. That bed, those sheets, Rick
smoking a cigarette, waiting for me to walk through the
door. I think about calling room #213 . . . *Rick, wait.* Is there
time for me to run to the end of the corridor, take the elevator to the lobby, rush to my car, drive to the interstate?

But today, at noon, the room will be vacant.

———

At twelve-thirty the lounge begins to empty. Parents and husbands retrieve raincoats and umbrellas. Without the crowd of people, the air-conditioning seems colder. I return to my room for a sweatshirt. I sit on my bed, forgetting to put it on.

I'm lying down when I hear a faint rap. I open my eyes and sit up. Ted. It's after three. The rain has stopped. Sunlight, pouring through the window, splashes the floor. A pair of sunglasses is hooked onto the neck of his faded T-shirt. Sweat dampens the material. The shirt isn't tucked into his jeans, ripped at the left knee. These are not the kind of clothes he wears to work, but since sometimes he works on weekends, this is his day off.

"I heard Andrew didn't show up," he says. "I'm sorry." He pushes the door wider, standing just inside the room. "I've got a few minutes. You want to talk?" He removes a bandanna from his pocket and wipes his forehead.

I don't want to see him like this: sweaty. I don't want to see the faint shadow of his kneecap behind the rip. I don't want to see the copper hair on his forearms. I barely want to see him at all. I don't want him to be male. I don't really want him to be human. I don't want to care for him too much.

"I can't talk to you like this," I say. "Why don't you just go?"

No, don't go.

He watches me for a moment. "Like what?"

"Well, dressed like that," I say.

I'm scared to see you dressed like that. I'm scared to think of you having a body. I don't want you to be a man who sweats.

"It's my day off," he says. "I was at the gym playing volley-ball." I turn my back to him and go to the window. Puddles in the parking lot steam in the heat of asphalt and sun. "What scares you?" he asks.

I shrug, still not looking at him. I watch a man, another man, a doctor in a white jacket with a stethoscope around his neck, walk past a row of cars and open the door to his Jeep. I wonder where he's going. I think about going with him. . . .

"Nothing does," I say.

"Sounds like you're angry. Why not get angry at your addict rather than me?"

I whirl around. "I'm angry because you look like . . ."

"What?"

"I don't know—a *man*."

"Try to see *me*. Not an object. I'm a man who won't hurt you or abandon you. I'd be angry, too, and frightened, not to be able to talk to someone who cares about *you*—and *not* your addict."

"I only know how to talk to men about *sex*."

"Your *addict* only knows how to talk about sex." He nods toward my Workbook on the nightstand, suggesting I do the exercise where I'm to write a description of my addict. "I think that'll help you see its power," he adds. "And will help you diminish it."

He turns to go. Quickly, I call him back.

He pauses, nodding.

Again, I think about what I learned from writing last night: that all I really wanted was to live—not just with Forrest, but with Shirley and Scottie, with a family. And Rick—that day at his house—I wanted to care for his sick son. I never figured out how to do something that simple. That hard.

"I think maybe my whole life has been a mistake," I whisper.

He takes a deep breath. "You were hurt. Be patient with yourself. You *will* get better."

"But . . . I really believe a man will never love *me*, or even *like* me, unless I have sex with him."

"I like you."

"You don't count!"

Ted smiles. "Thanks a lot."

After he leaves, I look out the window again. A moment later Ted crosses the lot.

Volleyball.

Ted plays volleyball on Thursdays. I obsess about men on Thursdays. I meet men in motels on Thursdays.

Ted, when he stood in the doorway, looked too alive, full of life. To play volleyball on Thursday is to choose life.

I'm jealous, I think.

But, okay, I can do this. I can do ordinary things, too.

I pick up the phone. Maybe Andrew forgot about visiting day. Maybe he got absorbed grading papers. I need to tell him who I am now—well, the woman I'm becoming. The phone begins to ring. No answer. We don't have an answering machine. I let it continue ringing. I wish my cat, Quizzle, could answer. I want to hear her purr. I want to throw ping-pong balls across the floor and let her chase them, her favorite game. I imagine my house. The velvet couch. All Andrew's books. The hat rack with his Atlanta Braves baseball cap.

Still no answer. No one home.

I am not an ordinary woman.

He doesn't want to see this unordinary woman here in the hospital.

He doesn't see me at home, either. Yes, I told him the reason I was coming here to the hospital was to attend to an eating disorder. Yet . . . just a month or so ago he walked into my bedroom and saw me reading a book on sex addiction, a book Ted had loaned me.

Andrew never asked about it.

I've also mentioned to him, seemingly casually, that I might have a few sexual issues to work out.

He never asked questions about this, either.

Just like he never asks about my addict clothes. Or where I disappear to on Thursdays. Why dinner (such as it is) is always late Thursday evenings.

He doesn't see what he sees . . . or know what he knows.

Andrew: a conveniently remote and distant husband. I deliberately selected him, my addict deliberately chose him, to ensure it has an excuse for an affair, an excuse to act out. *My husband doesn't see me. Therefore, I need you and you and you to make me feel better.*

I always thought I didn't want him to see me, didn't want

him to know. Except I drop so many hints, leave so many clues. Clothes. Flirting with men at parties. Letters from men appear in our post office box—and he usually picks up the mail. A trail of clues leading straight to this addiction.

Maybe I want him to discover me. Find me. I can confess. Be forgiven. Maybe I want this . . . as much as it terrifies me.

Suddenly I realize I can't remember the color of Andrew's eyes. Okay, not brown. Greenish? Kind of gray-green?

So—maybe I don't see or know *him*, either.

Maybe Andrew didn't show up today because he thinks I don't see him.

I *don't* see him.

Maybe he's angry I don't pay enough attention to him.

I *don't* pay enough attention to him.

So many issues: the addiction, my family, men, me. How can I try to save my marriage when I can barely save myself?

WORKBOOK

I open the Workbook to the section Ted told me about, where I'm to write a description of my addict.

I write: *Liquid hot steel night wild dark ice steaming, voice dying, like you could melt glass bone hard, devour a blue universe, prisoner for eternity.*

This image inhabits my mind. Sometimes it remains covert and seething. Other times it is the impetus, the mental stimulus that ultimately results in overt bad behavior.

This image has always been with me. Even as a child,

bored with the ordinary, bored with school, bored with childhood games, bored with friends who aren't truly boring, I mentally evaporate from my surroundings. I appear before you, and I am skilled at seeming to be present, but I am not present. As teachers discuss history, as girls discuss boys, I am in a *liquid hot steel night wild dark* . . . where effaced men breathe shadows, where air is harder than grit, and where I crave these men, romanticize them. Believe I love them.

It is danger hot enough to melt bone, rageful and wild enough to devour a peaceful blue universe. It imprisons me for eternity.

What does it take for mayhem of the mind to emerge into behavior? What does it take to reach territories so distant there is no turning back? What is the flash point, the confluence of forces that slam together at that irretrievable moment? A crescent moon on the wane, doldrums flattening over the equator, the Gulf Stream rising, glaciers cracking . . . just as we think about squeezing a trigger, just as we lust for a glint of a knife on the first frigid night of the year.

My own flash point is not just a dangerous man discovering my body. When my flash point is seconds from igniting, I will also find you, the predator with radar capable of discovering the one "me" in order for *your own* liquid hot steel night to become reality. The selection is not random. With one scent you know who I am. With one scent of you, my most trusted senses convince me to go with you.

And I must go.

For I have not learned to read or translate environments accurately. Harsh whispers of wind seep under doors, and I believe the breeze is gentle. No sane thought can find me. My heart is sealed from my mind. Stars are snuffed out across my liquid hot steel sky . . . while my breath is a drugged pulse, dying. I am grafted to night, to *your* night, dulled by sounds until all I can hear is a dangerous man's name.

Yet I am not a victim.

I am a predator.

I am not your victim because you are not a predator any more than a bottle of scotch stalks an alcoholic.

There are no victims.

We are men without mothers and girls with serial fathers. Repeat offenders.

No one here gets out alive.

In my liquid hot steel nights I must must must endlessly duplicate the familiarity of my dangerous childhood as closely as possible . . . re-create a past that scratches like the blade of a razor, a slit that is thin, but deep.

"His orgasm is more important than your life."

A therapist I once saw on television explained Jeffrey Dahmer, the serial killer and cannibal from Milwaukee, in this manner. He is the ultimate mayhem of liquid hot steel nights of addictive rage.

What is his flash point?

In a specific bar he meets a specific kind of man on a specific kind of night who reminds him of his soul's devastation.

He must lure this man home: to kill him; to eat him. Because the only way for Dahmer to feel loved or to live a nourishing life is for him to eat his companion.

Cannibalism, therefore, is the ultimate eating disorder. Since, in a food addiction, food is a substitute for spirituality, then Jeffrey Dahmer, who once worked in a chocolate factory, is the most destitute, the hungriest, the most spiritually starved of all.

He devours love. He devours sex. He wants to control and dominate and devour you. He boils flesh from bone. He chews slowly, swallowing body parts, in order to absorb them into his own being. He stores heads in his freezer, mementos from dates, killing his lovers so they won't leave him, eating his lovers to prevent abandonment. His most cherished souvenirs are Polaroids of dismembered bodies. He is a lover craving not Chanel No. 5 but the scent of blood. He collects body parts the way I collect maroon scarves, books by rageful writers . . . the way Rick will always treasure that photo of me.

Why the repetition? The serial? Surely the rehearsed, imagined fantasy is more enticing, more intriguing than the actual act. Nevertheless, from that fantasy, actual crimes and seductions are implemented as if following a script. Except the event is never as perfect as the controlled version in our heads. We must try the kill, the seduction, the binge, again and again, this time hoping to get it perfect. Just one more time and the conquest, the fuck, the murder, the kiss, the rape, will be the one perfect event in a life.

Except it isn't.

Something's not quite right.

Since *all* addicts are serial, the ritual must begin again. The fuck, the murder, the bottle of scotch, the Oreo cookie, do not provide everlasting love or solace, so we must try it, hope for it, with the next seductive fuck, murder, drink, piece of cake. Just one more time. Again and again.

Even though next time might push us over the edge. Even though next time we might fall into a vat of liquid hot steel and never recover.

If an ultimate fix is to control/destroy/seduce the world, then murderers, rapists, terrorists are the extreme addicts.

But you—you who do not murder or maim, what do *you* do when it's too painful to hear what you don't want to know? What is your drug of choice in this landscape zoned for addiction? Is your addictive rage turned outward on others? Do you turn it inward on yourself, mayhem minus behavior? There is a continuum of bad behavior, but the impulse is the same.

I murder my lover therefore I am.

I shop therefore I am.

I eat therefore I am.

I don't eat therefore I am not.

I am bulimic therefore I both am and am not.

I am powerful, wealthy, famous, therefore I am.

I am addicted to the powerful, the wealthy, the famous, therefore I am . . . or am not, fantasizing celebrities' lives in order to ignore my own.

I fuck therefore I am.

SEX FOOD MONEY MAYHEM
IS (ARE)
HERE
EVERY
DAY♠

We see the world with eyes closed and mouths open. Feed me. Feed my hungry heart until I feel better. Feed me until I am hungover. Then feed me again. Until I am drunk or unconscious. You can feed me anything as long as you call it love. Or happiness. Or success. Even though our kind of love lasts only as long as it takes for the word *sex* to be spoken. Even though our kind of happiness insists reality be stricken from the record.

We hear the message of sex in subliminal whispers as well as bombarded across airwaves. We smell it, hear it, touch it, taste it: in movies and music, in advertisements selling cars, cigarettes, clothes, alcohol, makeup, soap.

We sexualize nature, are taught to believe setting suns and moonlit beaches cannot be noticed unless we are lovers.

There is no escape from sex. It is a machine razing our minds, our vocabularies, our bodies.

Addiction lays our souls bare for an *invasion of the body snatchers*. All our nights are *nights of the living dead*.

We crave the artificial, the spangly glitz of addiction.

Swallow a potion: SEX. Smooth a balm on your skin: SUCCESS. Instant. Luscious. Inhale Elixir of Happiness. All I need to be gratified is a charm, a balm, an unguent, a pill, a wink, a glance, a smile. Desire. Love medicine. "Love Potion Number Nine."

DAY
EIGHT

RESOLUTELY, DAY AFTER DAY, I follow the regimen. Now I wake moments before six and am out of bed before Nancy knocks on the door. With determined steps I circle the hospital for twenty minutes. Eat what's placed on my plate. Attend group therapy every day. Individual sessions with Ted. Our group plans outings to the High Museum of Art and ZooAtlanta. We're driven to 12-Step groups to attend meetings of Overeaters Anonymous and Sex Addicts Anonymous. We write out our First Steps in the Workbook.

ART GROUP

We're to cut photographs from magazines that represent our ideal futures.

In a *National Geographic* I find a scene of a distant mountain. I want to transport myself into the print. Snow, stillness, serenity. Maybe this is the answer. I'll journey to a distant land where I'll never have to think or feel, where no one, nothing, not even a man could find me, touch me, tempt me. Live alone on that isolated mountaintop suspended in cold, empty air. A state of nothingness: I won't be drunk; nor will I have to struggle so hard to be sober.

Yet Ted says addicts live in just such extremes. In a confusion of people or total isolation. All or nothing. Gorging or abstaining. Addicted to food, addicted to starvation. Wanting every man or no man. Accomplishing everything—a seeming total success—or accomplishing little or nothing, a failure. The word *moderation*, Ted has told me, isn't part of an addict's vocabulary.

There must be a different way. . . .

I think about another picture I saw in a magazine several years ago. It was a photograph of the feminist Gloria Steinem, in an article about *Ms.* magazine, and her independent life *without a man*. I was in awe. Now I wonder: maybe I want what she has. Even as I have no idea how to obtain it.

Yet I have held jobs, various professional positions. I've worked on Capitol Hill for a congressman and two different senators. After I left Washington I wrote and edited a newsletter for a historical preservation organization. I worked for a zoological society. A few years ago I even went back to school to earn a master of fine arts degree in creative writing.

At my jobs I dressed in business clothes and acted professionally. No co-worker ever guessed the secret life I led. I always showed up on time. I received praise for my job performance and skills. Yet (unlike Gloria Steinem) the job, the education, the degree—life—were never as important or as interesting to me as a man.

After we finish cutting out pictures of our ideal futures, we tape them to the walls of the lounge. There are photos of expensive houses. Happy families eating breakfast together, large bowls of Wheaties. A couple on a sailboat in the tropics. An ad for Publishers Clearinghouse, a van stopping at a house offering champagne, balloons, ten million dollars. Drunk on money, sun, fun. We still struggle to discover what we really need or want.

BODY IMAGE GROUP

I lie on the floor in the group room, my arms by my sides, my legs flat, my eyes closed. Layer by layer, strip by strip, Linda places papier-mâché across my face, forming a mold. I'm soothed and comforted, hidden behind this tangible mask. Linda's fingers brush my forehead, chin, the bridge of my nose. Even though my mouth isn't covered, I don't speak. The room is quiet. All the women, partnered, surround me. I feel as if I'm disappearing behind gluey strips of paper.

As the paper and glue harden, Nancy, the nurse, talks about masks. She wants us to think of our addiction and the different masks we wear that keep our true selves hidden. Her voice is steady, direct, clear.

When Linda is finished, I grip the sides of the mask and pull. It tugs at my skin. Like the addict mask, more difficult to remove than it seems. I place it on the floor in front of me. Of course, it doesn't really look like me, but still I stare at this mold in the shape of my face. I trace a finger around the eyes, the mouth.

Nancy turns to each of us, asking: *What do you see? What do people see when they look at your face? What do you want them to notice?*

The masks of the addict are varied. We switch to an addict "face" as easily as we change expression. I am *all* pretense, a palimpsest, like these strips of papier-mâché. I hide beneath layer after layer of lies, secrets, different lives: the Rainbow Motel image I show Rick; the pretend-I'm-normal mask I show friends; the pretend-I'm-professional mask I've shown co-workers; the pretend-I'm-a-wife mask I show Andrew.

This exercise is a ritual. Masks suffocate. Remove the layers. Remove the masks. The false personas. Remove the addiction.

I look at Nancy. Gray threads her dark hair. Her gaze is no-nonsense. Direct. She wears a simple gold wedding band on her left hand. I imagine she has cookouts on Labor Day and the Fourth of July. She probably plans Thanksgiving dinner weeks in advance. I want to ask her how she does this. I want to ask her what she and her husband talk about over dinner every night. Why does nothing lure her out of her house after midnight? How is she brave enough to be pale and ordinary?

Later in the day Nancy brings a mirror and makeup into the group room. She hands out lip gloss, mascara, blush, and teaches us to apply makeup for *ourselves*, not for men. She instructs us to look at ourselves in the mirror with our *own* eyes, without wondering what a man sees. I open a tube of Raspberry Glacé. Just the scent, the color, the syllables, remind me of . . . everything I'm supposed to forget.

"Pretend you're walking down the beach, alone, wearing lipstick," she says to me. "Just hold that image, keep thinking it, over and over. *You're on the beach. You're alone.*"

Imprint my mind with new images, colors, scents, sights. A new me.

And for an hour or more I can do this. But tonight Gabriel is to drive us to a 12-Step group. Men.

At dinner, I place food in my mouth carefully, so as not to disturb the Raspberry Glacé.

In a hospital van, Gabriel drives us to a meeting of Sex Addicts Anonymous—SAA—to get sponsors, contacts and phone numbers, a schedule of meetings, so we will be prepared when we leave the hospital. Part of the search, too, is for a Higher Power, a spiritual force stronger than the addiction.

A man stands at the front of a meeting room in the basement of a church explaining the program: it is for men and women who want to recover from their own sexual addiction, as well as offer their experience, strength, and hope to help others recover. It is up to us, individually, to decide how to express our sexuality in ways that will not hurt us mentally, physically, spiritually.

When the man finishes speaking, we split into groups for check-in, pulling metal chairs into two circles. In this room with men, my mask with raspberry lips slips into place. I must—I glance around the room—I must pull my chair next to . . . which man? You, Man . . . in the seersucker suit. I sit next to you. I want to meet you, you must notice me, even in baggy shorts and ripped T-shirt.

"My name is Ed, and I'm a sex addict."

"Hi, Ed," we intone.

Ed, in a gray suit and bow tie. . . .

It is early September, still warm in Georgia. The room feels close and still. There is no air-conditioning, just a fan, and I think I smell men sweating. It reminds me of Gabriel sweating, that night he woke me.

". . . Then when I went out of town on business," Ed is saying, "I deliberately didn't put the chain lock on the door of my hotel room. So the next morning, when the maid came to clean, I made sure I was in the bathroom with only a towel. Of course, I acted surprised and embarrassed. But meanwhile, my addict got real jazzed when she saw me like that. Then I masturbated.

"Except now . . ." Ed straightens his bow tie. "I can't believe I did it. I feel like one of those sleazy flashers in a trench coat. I want to pretend, since I'm a business executive, that I'm not like that. But I *am*."

When he stops speaking, throats clear, chairs creak.

"Hi, I'm Ginger." Ginger's eyes, with the hard glitter of addiction, suggest she hasn't been in recovery long. "I feel like I'm addicted to everything," she says. A small laugh of recognition ripples through the group. "For one thing, I'm addicted to husbands. I've had four. But I'm also addicted to money, television, talking on the phone, gossip. Every time a friend calls to tell me about a problem she's having, or whatever, all I can think of, even while she's still talking, is telling someone else *her* news. And I know it's costing me friendships. But I can't stop.

"I also do this strange thing. It's hard to explain—but like when I pass that S & M Auto Supply place up on the highway, I *always* think of sadomasochism. Or, you know all those Georgia license plates that have that prefix 'SFX'? I always think of 'SEX' when I see them. Stuff like that. Honestly, about all I'm not addicted to are broccoli and spirituality."

She pauses. The hardness in her eyes softens. Then she talks about her childhood, how her addiction began because her mother used to hit her. To numb out she became compulsive, about small stuff at first. "Like all day at school I'd obsess about what kind of candy to buy on my way home, licorice or Hershey's kisses. Later, when I got older, I'd lie in bed—not just masturbating—but kind of stroking myself to feel better. This whole addiction just began as comfort."

"Hi, my name is Jim and I'm a recovering sex addict."

Jim . . . the man I sit beside in the seersucker suit and white shirt, open at the collar, and gold wire-rimmed glasses.

His brown hair is short, his nose thin and straight, his eyes pale green, the color of limes.

"I'm still acting out," he says. "Well, I'm not actually having sex, but I'm still into crazy thinking. Yesterday, I was stopped at a traffic light, and there was this girl in a red Camaro in the next lane. And it's like I imagined smiling at her and having sex with her, and that she would love having sex with me. I mean, just like that." He snaps his fingers. "I got so into this thing, just in one minute or so at the stoplight, that I even imagined what it would be like *marrying* her. And the marriage ceremony. Her wedding dress. My tux.

"But then the light turned green. She turned left and I went straight ahead and I actually *missed* her. I wanted to follow her. It didn't matter where she was driving, where she was going, whether she was already married or not. I couldn't get her out of my head. I still miss her." He pauses. "Guess that's all," he says. "Pass it on."

Jim . . . in a gray tux. I am in ivory lace and satin buttons. I clasp a bouquet of white roses and walk down the aisle on a velvet runner. To Jim. Where he waits. For me. . . .

"My turn. I'm Don and I guess I'm a sex addict.

"My wife had a baby about thirteen months ago and I can't stand having sex with her anymore." Don's voice, a monotone, sounds disconnected from the words. "I can't even look at her anymore, you know, at her body. I don't understand—it disgusts me. And I feel so guilty." In shame, he stares at his feet.

"But my mother—I guess this's the really guilty part—

used to come and kiss me good night wearing this sheer nightgown. She smelled so good. And she sat on my bed and held my shoulders and kissed me on the mouth. Just quick-like. But still. After she left, I'd think about her and some-times my thoughts were scary. I'd kind of fantasize about her while I touched myself. I know how disgusting that sounds—but I did. I thought I was bad and perverted. I was always so ashamed. So now, just thinking about my wife—who's a *mother*—all this shame comes back up. You know—since my wife's a mother now, she reminds me of my own."

"I'm Vicki. I've been sober two years. And it's so great to see the *real* world, finally. I'm dating a guy, three months, and we haven't had sex yet. We're really trying to get to know each other as friends first. Learn to talk and be honest with our feelings. So far it's working. I'm surprised. I always told myself the *only* way to get close to a man was with sex. But I never knew any of those men the way I know this boyfriend."

Vicki crosses her legs. Her panty hose are without runs or snags, nor do they bag around her ankles. The part through her short hair is straight, and her white cotton blouse is crisp, without wrinkles. "And I planted a small oak tree in my backyard," she continues. "As a Higher Power. I want to feel its energy as we both grow together."

Several people in the group glare at Vicki as she speaks, at her upbeat, cheery recovery.

"Hi, my name is Linda, and I'm a love addict. Or a code-pendent sex addict. Or a romance addict." She smiles. "Or all of the above."

I'm surprised that Linda, in a lavender gypsy dress, has chosen to speak.

"I feel like giving up," she says. She opens her purse and removes a tissue. "My two children are anorexic. My husband is addicted to prescription drugs, but since he's a respected doctor, we all pretend it's not a problem. So he blames me for everything wrong in our family. And I don't know, maybe he's right." She leans forward and stares at the floor, the tissue grasped in her hands.

"I lost my job because my boss's wife found out I was fucking her husband," Linda continues. "We've been having an affair for over a year. I've only ever even had two or so affairs, but I feel like the original Velcro woman. I mean, I can't ever break up with the man or let go. And this man, my former boss, he'll never leave his wife, but I don't want to lose him. I *love* him. And I know how crazy that sounds, but I don't think I can live without him.

"I mean, I know, my therapist tells me, I just 'use' him like a distraction to numb out. To avoid dealing with the fact that my marriage and my life are a mess. Sometimes—this sounds awful—but I'd stay late at work to be with him, rather than go home and fix dinner for my kids. This's all so scary. I really need help. I guess I need a sponsor, too. And some phone numbers for when I get out of the hospital. After the meeting if anyone wants to give me some. Thanks."

I glance at my watch. A few minutes before nine. Almost time for the meeting to end.

A man with red hair and a blue tie doesn't introduce himself. He can barely speak. We all stop fidgeting and shuffling, our eyes riveted to his face. "I've lost my family," he whispers. "My wife. She took our son and moved out." He takes a deep breath and presses his palms to the sides of his face. "I masturbate. That's what I—I do. And I . . . did this awful thing. I videotaped it. And my son. He's seven. I left the tape lying around. He . . ."

The man stops speaking. No one else claims time. It is like a moment of silence for a wounded son, a wounded father, a wounded family, a wounded life.

With all of us—I know—it's only when we're high that we feel indestructible. Here, now, we know we're not. Here, now, we know we eat ourselves to death. Starve ourselves to death. Drink ourselves to death. Fuck ourselves to death. Slow suicide. Sexual suicide. Suicide of the soul. Waiting for the body to follow.

I am dizzy with the words of everyone's story—even though I had not intended to listen to anyone. I had believed that our secret words would sound like a wind you can't hear, gusting along deserted pathways of understanding, because the addict dwells in no terrain of living language.

Except. I glance at the man with the red hair and the blue tie. I try to imagine his son. I try to imagine all the abandoned wives, children, husbands, lovers.

I try to imagine all the cool glass hearts. I try to imagine the sound of glass cracking. As much as before, at the beginning of the meeting, I didn't want to speak, now I think maybe I should say something—even one sentence.

Except, I want my own heart to remain cool and rigid.

I lean my elbows on my knees, clasp my hands together, and break out in a sweat.

Gabriel, I need to speak your name. I can't say your name. I can't even say my own name. I can't explain who I am.

Except. I am Linda and the man with whom she had the affair. I am Jim as well as the girl in the red Camaro.

"There's this man," I finally whisper. I stare at my untied shoelaces. I hear the fan whirring. "We haven't had sex. So far we've just talked. I don't know if he's dangerous. He seems so, well, quiet." *And right now he's waiting outside in the van. All I really want is for this meeting to end so I can see him.* "I keep thinking," I add, "hoping . . . I want him to be who he seems. But I don't know if he is. I don't know if *I* am. I don't even know what I need." *I need him. I need to sit in the van beside him. No: I want to be with him in his silver truck.* "Maybe I just need to be here. Thanks."

Chairs are pushed back as the meeting ends. Jim leans close to me. I'm afraid to look at him. I'm afraid all I'll need is one nanosecond in which to fall madly in love with him. I do not release my clasped hands, scared my addictwoman will brush a hand along his shoulder. If I hear his voice I might touch him. I might even tell him *I* am the girl in the red Camaro.

"That guy you were talking about . . ." His voice is low. I barely hear him above the chatter of voices. I hold my breath as he speaks. I don't want to smell his cologne, scared I'll remember it forever. "Be careful," he says. "I've come on to women just by talking. They don't know I got this act. It's all an act. Years ago I realized there're lots of women I could seduce better with romantic fantasies than by serious sexual stuff. It's all a line. Even if it sounds like it isn't. Maybe especially if it sounds like it isn't."

A line of sweat has broken out above his lip. I grip my hands tighter. How easily I could touch that lip, wipe that sweat away with my finger. "Thank you," I say. "Thank you for telling me."

I stand to follow the other women from my unit up the stairs to the van—to Gabriel.

"Wait."

Jim stands a few steps behind me. He pushes at his wire-rimmed glasses as if they've slipped down the bridge of his nose. "Don't take this wrong. You know, I don't know if we're even supposed to be talking or anything. I haven't been coming here very long. But there's one other thing I want to say, about that man you mentioned." I nod. "I know you deserve better than him."

I'm unable to answer. I know if I talk with him one moment longer I will say: *You, Jim, could be better than him.* I know if I look at him one moment longer, I will follow *him* home.

When I return to my room after the SAA meeting, Jill stands in the middle of the floor surrounded by her three suitcases. Her face is raw and blotched as if permanently discolored by too much makeup. Her clothes hang loose on her body, which, while not frail, seems hollow, as if it's been scoured. Her smile, when she sees me, is evasive, shy, almost embarrassed. Odd I didn't notice this before she left: her front teeth are gray. Bulimic gray. Tarnished from years of vomit.

"I broke one of my damn fingernails," she says, picking at it. Her voice sounds hoarse from cigarette smoke and damp bars. "It made me so mad."

"That's why you came back?"

"Yeah, right. Work through the fucking anger." Lifting one foot at a time, she kicks her high-heeled shoes across the floor.

I sink onto my bed, smiling, yet not sure whether I'm pleased to see her or not.

Nancy comes in and gives Jill a paper cup for a urine specimen.

"What you check for in this place, anyway?" Jill says. "Alcohol? Drugs? Traces of semen? You do a fat count? See if I've been bingeing on doughnuts?"

"Just do it," Nancy says. "I'm going to check your things."

Jill goes to the bathroom and Nancy unzips each of Jill's suitcases. She removes shirts, underwear, slips, slacks, dresses. She unfastens each cosmetics bag and flips open compacts and tubes of lipstick. She inhales containers of body lotion and perfume. She searches pockets, rolls socks inside out, and slips her hand into the toe of each shoe.

She checks for contraband—not just alcohol or drugs. She checks for cookie crumbs and sticks of gum. We are not allowed Lifesavers or breath mints. No cigarettes, laxatives, aspirin, vitamins, antacids, mouthwash. Anything that can be placed in our mouths—as a "drug"—except toothpaste, is

forbidden. And we're only allowed to use toothpaste spar-
ingly. One lone strawberry Lifesaver, sewn into the hem of a
dress like a ruby, would be confiscated and flushed down the
toilet.

Jill seems to be clean. She has not hidden illegal cough
drops in her deepest shirt pocket or a stick of gum in the toe
of a shoe. But even though they discovered my razor blade,
how easily I slipped Forrest's maroon scarf onto the unit in
my suitcase (like an alcoholic smuggling scotch into detox),
because no one knew the scarf was a drug.

Jill returns and hands the cup to Nancy, who leaves. From
Jill's desk drawer I remove her cards and photos and hold up
the photo of the little girl in the Brownie uniform, her hair
in pigtails, her front tooth missing. "Cute kid," I say.

She takes it from me and tosses it on the desk, face down.

"Christ, Jill. I say, 'Cute kid.' You say, 'Thank you.' Or,
'That's my sister in first grade.' Or—"

"Jesse's only my kid sister."

I sit back down on my bed and bunch the pillow against
my stomach. "Oh. Where does she live?"

"Who knows? Who cares?" I suspect that while she may
not know where her sister is, she *does* care. "I don't want to
talk about it. I don't much want to talk about anything."

"Gosh, it's really great having you back," I say. "Why'd you
even bother?"

"Because I knew how much you all must've missed me."
She arranges her mirror and makeup on the desk. "Didn't
you try calling?" She pauses, looks up.

She wants to know whether I called that wrong number she gave me. "No," I lie, my face blank. "Figure we didn't have much to say."

All the features on her face are still. I almost think she's disappointed—though she'd never admit it. And in this quiet moment, I think it might have been a mistake to lie. But I don't want to be vulnerable, am too scared to tell the truth. We both are.

"So—guess it didn't go so great out there," I say, changing the subject.

She turns her back to me and switches on the pink mirror lights. "Decided my Higher Power was the CEO of Anheuser-Busch. You know—bars, hot-sheet motels. Another count-to-ten-and-I'm-gone relationship."

"Good career move."

"Yeah, well, now that I'm back and have to deal with that *Nancy* . . ." She sighs. "Drunk off my ass just *feels* so much better than sober."

"That's because 'drunk' doesn't have any real feelings, period."

"Reality isn't all it's cracked up to be, either. Who can stay sober forever?" She reapplies mascara and eyeliner. "I mean, when I stop drinking I start eating. When I stop eating I start fucking. Or I feel like buying every pair of shoes in Macy's." She smooths crimson gloss across her lips, then smiles at herself in the mirror.

That smile. Those teeth. "Or you vomit it all up," I say.

Her lips compress. The corners of her eyes narrow. Yet her mirrored gaze remains latched on mine—not wanting me to

know I touched her core of shame. Not men. Not sex. Not
alcohol. Rather, shadowy teeth that look like the smudge of
an eraser.

She blinks. The blink is silent, of course, yet seems percussive—yes, like shame.

"So what?" she says. "It's a compromise."

"Get to have your cake and not eat it, too."

She jams her feet back in her heels and heads toward the
door.

"Where you going?" It's after ten.

"Thought I'd see if Gabriel's around."

No. Don't go. You can't talk to him. *I* talk to him. He's *my*
compromise. Don't you want to talk to me?

"Thought I'd see if *he* missed me," she adds.

But he *can't* have missed her. How can he want her with
her gray teeth?

She leaves the room. Again, I pick up the photograph of
Jesse, her sister. My sister, Kiki, who knows where I am, here
in the hospital, hasn't called to see how I am . . . but I want
to believe she cares for me, too, even though it's so difficult
for her—always—to show it.

Back when we both lived in Boston I remember one day,
during the period when I was still seeing Forrest, sitting on
the couch in her living room. Kiki, two years older than I,
waits for her husband to return from the science lab where
he's working on a Ph.D. They have tickets for a concert; I am
to baby-sit my nephew, napping in the next room. I give my
sister a belated Christmas present. She takes the package and

drops it on the kitchen counter, saying she'll open it later. The present is a pair of silver earrings with small lapis lazuli stones. Yet I know that this gift, like all others, scares her, as if binding her in a small commitment to the giver. And I give presents to her still hoping, after all these years, I will discover the one perfect gift that *will* bind her to me, even if for just a moment.

I timed my arrival to coincide with a radio program on which Forrest is being interviewed. His voice is low background music to Kiki rustling around the rooms. She washes dishes, hangs up clothes, tosses away magazines, letters, papers—hiding evidence that any one specific person lives in her house. I see no teething rings, no rattles or stuffed animals, no baby pictures, no afghans, no man's slippers or ties or belts. No evidence of baby, husband, wife, or mother. My sister discards even the smallest amount of clutter; to her, life is clutter.

Even as the rooms are spotless, there is no congruent whole. Paintings and prints are haphazardly placed. A chair here, a throw rug there, no cozy corner where you could curl up and read a book.

The room is too chilly for concentration on a book.

I would ask my sister to turn up the heat except I know she'll refuse. Nor do I tell her I'm cold. I wouldn't want her to know I'm uncomfortable, for I believe this would please her. It would mean she is tougher, sturdier, healthier than I am.

Forrest, his voice distant and full of static, expresses concern that Communist sympathizers are infiltrating the Vietnam peace movement, the student protesters. I want to tell my sister why I listen to him. I also want to tell her how our father looked at me, as if I were a stranger, when I was home during Christmas vacation. But even if she stopped rushing around the house long enough to sit beside me, I wouldn't be able to speak to her. She slides through all conversations with light, airy phrases, weightless, almost slick. She can't hear my words; nor does she speak words that stick.

We never talk about our childhoods, either, almost as if we were raised in separate families, hybrid sisters. In a way we are. I have only vague memories of her growing up. She was always out with friends—or just out. To her, anywhere else was better than home. And while it was true, that anywhere else *was* better, still, I always wanted to stop her, so she'd stay home with *me*. I wanted to be weighted by a sister's presence. *Do you want to play a card game? Do you want me to rub your back?*—I always asked—trying to delay her departure before she slammed out the door. Her passage through our childhoods was thin, as thin as her body, not wanting anyone to see her, notice her, hold on to her.

I barely listen to Forrest's interview. Whether Communists are in the peace movement or not doesn't interest me. I listen because, regardless of what he says, I want to believe he speaks only to me, that I am the sole recipient of his voice, and that I will be able to decode a secret message. In his tone, in pauses between sentences and thoughts, I know he thinks of me, even as he speaks of something else.

Kiki, efficiently clasping her son in one arm, a high chair in the opposite hand, his security blanket tucked in the crook of her elbow, drops the chair in the middle of the room and deposits him onto the seat. She puts his frayed blue blanket on the tray. Quickly he clasps it and sticks a corner of it in his mouth, along with his thumb. He has large solemn blue-gray eyes, still slightly unfocused and drowsy from his nap.

"What're you listening to that shit for?" she says. "What an idiot—people who see Communists under beds."

I've always thought of her as *my* beautiful sister, *the* beautiful sister, with light blue eyes, dark eyebrows, delicate nose, full lips. She needs no ornamentation and wears jeans, a coarsely knit pullover sweater, loafers, and thick socks. A narrow wedding band. Her long hair is in a loose bun. While she is skinny, she is not frail, her frame a sturdy scaffold that will not quake or be disturbed either by tears or by unbridled joy.

I shrug. "He's a friend."

"Him?" She nods toward the radio, now slightly impressed that I know someone being interviewed, whether he's an idiot or not. "How?"

"I was kind of working for him for a while."

"What for? You don't need money."

"Kind of as a friend."

Now I have her attention. She pauses in the doorway between the living room and kitchen. "No kidding," she says, her expression coolly nuanced.

Her gaze lingers on my face, possibly the longest I have ever been imprinted onto her consciousness. Usually when we speak, she either glances just past my head or else busies herself with ironing or washing dishes. Now, I can tell, she tries to determine whether I mean the word *friend* literally or euphemistically. She also tries to determine, I suspect, who this sister is who might attract a man important enough to be interviewed on the radio. If I am anything at all to her, I am only a younger sister who's murky and secretive. While she would never glimpse my film noir image, she has no other image, either. In fact, now I wish she would ask me what I mean by the word *friend*. I want her, *my* older sister, to warn me about married men, older men, urge me to stay away from a man who would have sex with a girl young enough to be his daughter.

"I think, maybe, I kind of like him," I whisper. "Maybe a lot. But he's kind of married."

"Live it up while it lasts," she says. "But don't get your hopes up. He'll never leave his wife for you."

I watch my nephew suck the corner of his blanket.

A car horn honks. Kiki grabs a jacket, tells me to feed him a jar of strained apricots.

Forrest's interview is over. I switch off the radio and turn the heat up to seventy degrees. I pull my nephew's high chair next to the kitchen window and sit in front of him. I open the jar of apricots. I dip a small silver spoon into it and nudge it against his lips. A corner of his blanket remains gripped in his fist. I've never heard him cry, as if he already knows no one is listening. He is quiet, seems tentative, as if waiting for something. Whatever it is, I believe he will have to wait a long time.

I feel quiet and tentative in his presence myself. I hold him, burp him, gently place him back in his crib, worried

he'll break. Even in the imbricated layers of family, genera-
tions, inheritances, I worry the layers won't protect him; in
fact, he should be protected from these layers. I want to protect him.

In a family scrapbook is a photograph taken at the opening of my father's bank in New Jersey. We are all fashionably
dressed in fall outfits, my mother and sister wearing new
hats. My father stands between my mother and me, his arm
around me, his hand clamped on my elbow. I stare straight
into the camera, smiling. No one notices the slight strain that
begins in my shoulders and twists down my body, as if my
body senses a faint danger along the spine. My mother looks
neither at the camera nor at her family, apparently not sure
of her place in the family or in the world. My sister stands to
my mother's right, an empty space between her and the rest
of her family, clumped together. She smirks: she has escaped
this family. Only my father stands erect, his shoulders
relaxed, his smile thin but proud, proud of his family he has
created.

I pick up the photograph of Jill's sister one last time. I
wonder what family secrets this small girl has, what she
would say if she were brave enough to step from this photograph and speak.

10:40. Jill hasn't returned yet. I wonder if she found Gabriel
in the lounge. I wonder what they are doing. I wonder what
Gabriel is doing. Or Jim, home now, slowly removing his
seersucker suit. . . .

No. Stop these thoughts. Right now. Wait.

Men have always pulsed through my mind, unceasing. But now, this eighth day in the hospital, there are thin units of time during breakfast, say, or group therapy, or spirituality, art therapy, game time (addicts don't know how to relax, so we're instructed to play cards or board games), when the static of fantasies diminishes.

Like the other day, playing Monopoly, I land on Boardwalk, buy it, build hotels, collect money, and, in the joy of winning, I don't immediately associate hotels with the Rainbow Motel. Rather, it's as if for one moment I step outside my self and watch an unknown woman in an unfamiliar body perform one new unusually ordinary task: playing a game.

I lie down on top of the bedspread. I must practice how to refocus my mind, my senses. This is a test: see how long I can go without thinking about a man. I glance at the clock again. 10:45. I concentrate on the word *reduction*. Reduce sight to what is before me. Slowly my gaze trails around the room. Lingering here. Lingering there. One generic flower petal on the patterned curtains. Textured cinder-block walls, painted tan. White ceiling. Beige industrial carpet. No stains. The dresser drawers are shut. Prints of butterflies with specks of black on yellow scalloped wings. Tan vinyl chair. The thick wood door that would hush sound if I were allowed to shut it. (Doors must be partially open at all times, except when we're dressing.) The silver knob on the door, similar to every other doorknob in the universe. Ordinary. Familiar.

My gaze narrows. To my size-five-and-a-half feet. Fingers. Kneecaps. Why does this territory labeled "body," this geography of skin, cause such distraction and destruction? How can this same body now live in a hospital while it attempts to become a different body, learn different routines and movements?

None of the men would recognize me in the hospital. *What are you doing here?* they'd ask. *You're fine the way you are*, they'd say. Those men wouldn't recognize the woman I'm trying to become. Men.

Better if I don't notice my body.

11:10 P.M. The red plastic clock I brought from home has a Mickey Mouse face on the white dial. The red second hand clicks past Mickey's nose, smiling mouth, eyes, black mouse ears. One second. Five seconds. Ten. Twenty. If only I can stay the way I am right now for one more second. One more. Just until the second hand touches the top of Mickey's right ear.

DAY NINE

AT BREAKFAST, Linda, Jill, Sheila, and I sit together. This morning at weigh-in, the woman with the Ensure slammed her pole, now decorated with a pink ribbon, on the scale, refusing to weigh her own body. When Nancy insisted she get on the scale, the woman tried to rip the tubes from her nostrils. This was all I could stand to see. I hurried off, the first one for exercise. Now the woman has not appeared for breakfast. So far, as if in solidarity with the woman and her pole, I've eaten nothing. Sheila is not eating, either. She stares at the plate: eggs, two pieces of whole-wheat toast unbuttered, half a grapefruit.

Linda cuts her sunny-side-up eggs as well as her toast into

tiny pieces, ritualizing food before she eats it. Jill stuffs gobs of food into her mouth as if she's destroying evidence. The compulsion is to control food. We will decide not just *if*, but also *how* it will enter our bodies. When Jill finishes, she pushes her plate away and leans back in her chair.

"Would you hurry up?" she says to Sheila and me. "I hate the smell of breakfast."

Sheila, hunched over the table, over her untouched plate of food, begins to cry. She wears her usual black sweats as if her body's in mourning.

"What is it?" Linda asks. "What's wrong?"

Sheila has no tissue and wipes tears away with the back of her hand. "There isn't enough," she says.

"Enough what?" Linda asks.

"Food," Sheila says.

"You mean breakfast?" I say. I look at the untouched plate of food I'm required to finish, and think about giving it to Sheila.

"No," Sheila says. "There isn't enough food, period. Soon as I finish breakfast, it'll be gone. Then there won't be any more food until lunch. Then dinner. Then *that* food'll be gone. All I do after finishing breakfast is think about what I'll eat for lunch. Even when I'm home and can eat all the food in my house, there isn't enough."

What can we say to Sheila? She's right. There never is enough.

Even for the woman with the pole, there isn't enough.

Enough love. I know Ted would tell us it is love we're truly after—that we don't feel enough love, don't know how to love. We use sex, food, alcohol, money—external objects of false gratification—to try to fill inner emptiness, loss, need—in this emotionally purblind world. Only if Sheila learned to love herself, felt complete, would there be enough.

Nancy comes over to survey our plates. She tells Sheila and me to get started, breakfast is almost over.

"I'm not hungry," I say.

"You have to eat one hundred percent," she says. "That's the rule."

The eggs look cold and rubbery. "I thought we're supposed to decide things for ourselves now. Accept responsibility for our actions."

"You're here to *learn* how to do that." Nancy picks up my fork and hands it to me. "If you restrict, you're going to end up with a bag of Ensure."

"You stick that shit down my nose," Jill says, "I'm outta here."

"You girls think this is a spa and you can check in and out whenever you want?" Nancy says. "You need to start realizing these things can kill you. You starve yourselves, you can die of heart attacks. You don't use condoms, you can get STDs, or worse. You keep picking up strange men, one night you might get yourselves beaten or killed."

Slowly I begin to eat. One hundred percent.

"My whole life, all I ever wanted besides a man, was to be as thin as this." Linda is sitting on the vinyl chair in my room reading *Vogue*. It's midafternoon, free time, break time, and I sit on my bed leafing through the Workbook. Linda holds up a photograph of a model who looks about an ounce away from an autopsy.

"Pole Lady is fatter than that," Jill says. She sits before her mirror tweezing her eyebrows.

"I don't think she's going to make it," Linda says.

"At least she'll go out thin," Jill says.

"Jesus," I say.

"Well, she's so creepy," Jill says, "wheeling that fucking pole up and down the hall."

"I just wish she'd *eat*," I say. "Those tubes."

"At the very least she ought to *pretend* to eat," Jill says. "Fake it. She can always sneak in the bathroom and throw it up later."

"Don't you *ever* want to settle down and be the least bit normal?" I ask.

Jill puts down the tweezers and smooths a finger across her eyebrows. "No. Guess I was born with sand in my shoes."

"What's that mean?"

"Oh, something Gabriel told me." Her gaze finds mine in the mirror. "You know, keep moving. Don't stay put in one place too long."

"What else does Gabriel tell you?" I ask.

"Besides," Jill says, "even Saint Ted's not married."

"I hardly think you want to compare your life to his."

Linda rips a scented perfume advertisement from the magazine and wafts it through the air. At first I inhale it, wanting to hold on to the scent. But then I exhale. The scent reminds me of that other me.

"And what is it with all these fucking butterflies all over the place?" Jill nods toward the prints on the wall and toward the cover of my Workbook.

"You know, like us," Linda says. "This place is like a cocoon where we stay till we're ready to fly."

"This place has serious metaphor issues."

I find an insert in the Workbook from the National Council on Sexual Addiction/Compulsivity. It asks twenty questions in order to determine if you are a codependent sex addict— as opposed to just a sex addict. As if the label matters.

The answer "yes" to the following questions will let you know if you suffer from sexual co-dependency:

1. I am, or have been, in a relationship with a person I felt was a sex addict.
2. I am, or have been, in an ongoing relationship where I felt the person I was having sex with was fantasizing about having sex with someone else.
3. In a past or current relationship, I have felt degraded by a sexual behavior I was asked to perform or actually did perform.
4. I feel that I don't have a clear understanding of what normal sexual behavior is about.
5. I have been sexually abused or raped.
6. In my family, we did not discuss sex.
7. I currently use other substances to numb my feelings (e.g. alcohol, drugs, caffeine, nicotine, sugar, food or work).
8. I have gone back into a relationship I wanted to end

with a person who had sexually compulsive behavior.

9. During sex in a past or present relationship, I often felt used and/or controlled.

10. I have wondered if I myself might be a sexual addict.

11. My intuition has told me that a past or current committed partner was being sexually unfaithful but I denied it to stay in the relationship longer than what was good for myself.

12. I have searched through my partner's belongings looking for proof of their extracurricular sexual activity.

13. I have followed my partner around trying to catch them in another sexual relationship.

14. I have been in a relationship where my partner wanted to include pornographic material in the sexual relationship.

15. I have or had a partner who would consistently masturbate even after having sex regularly.

16. I find it hard to say no to people sexually.

17. I have tolerated sexually inappropriate behavior from a partner just to stay in a relationship and not be alone.

18. I have blamed my partner's extra sexual activity on the other person, not my partner.

19. I believe deep down I can be enough sexually for my partner and that I can change them or make them love me.

20. I have been or currently am in a relationship where no matter how much sex we have, my partner is not satisfied.

Yes. Yes. And yes.

Am I a sex addict? A codependent sex addict?

Regardless of the label, here in the hospital, I must learn to write, speak, think my way out of the addiction. I want to discover language that's truer than the euphemisms addicts employ in order to lull ourselves into believing that we don't see what we see, that we don't know what we know.

For example, the word *always* is crucial in the argot of addiction. If something is *always* done, then we pretend it's all right: "he's *always* been a heavy drinker"; "she's *always* eaten like a bird"; "he's *always* liked his food"; "I *always* eat only two meals a day"; "I *always* skip breakfast"; "I've *always* had a sweet tooth."

No: you're an alcoholic; you're addicted to starvation; you're addicted to food; you're addicted to sugar.

For male sex addicts, euphemism condones bad behavior: "what a stud"; "he sure is macho"; "boys will be boys, men will be men"; or, "you know how guys are."

Even though euphemism fails with women sex addicts, connotations don't, so words still deny truth. We are called whores, sluts, loose women, nymphomaniacs. Those of us involved with married men are "home wreckers," even though the husband is "acting like a man."

Or else the language of silence is spoken. Wives ignore their husbands' hidden bottles of vodka. Husbands ignore their wives' insatiable diets or stashes of candy bars. Parents don't see the stoned glaze in their kids' eyes. In this, even

Jeffrey Dahmer's family isn't much different from our own. Three years before Dahmer was caught, his family discovered a vat filled with bones and slime in his grandmother's house, where he was staying. The family couldn't tell if the bones were animal or human. Nothing was ever reported.

We speak a language anonymous as sexual graffiti. A language steeped in alchemy. We change *sex* to *love*, change *self* to *others*, *remembering* to *forgetting*. Addiction is language run amok.

DAY
TEN

MY HUSBAND AND I sit in the group room alone with Ted. Andrew is steady and stoic, but I believe this is just a pose, his protection, to keep me—this scary woman he married—distanced, unseen, unnoticed. He speaks to Ted about me as if I'm not present, as if I'm deaf, or else a horrifying creature too dangerous to acknowledge directly. Perhaps this creature is my addictwoman rattling around behind closed doors—out of sight, out of mind—in the upstairs bedroom.

Andrew's hand is on the armrest. I want to reach for it. I want to touch it, press it to my face, and let him feel me. I can't. If he touches me he'll feel marks from men's fingers and will know I'm unfaithful. Yet I also want to touch his hand hoping I will become him, or at least become *like* him—so unneedy, so steady—never someone who would crave another person.

Now he is explaining that he didn't come on visiting day because he feels discouraged. He thinks I'll be in an institution forever. Or, if not, then quarantined in my room in our house. No longer can he see me as a normal woman, an ordinary wife.

"What do you most want from her when she leaves here?" Ted asks Andrew.

"I want her to function." His voice sounds unforgiving. I don't blame him. For years he has chosen to live with my severe mood swings without understanding them. At times, when I'm acting out my addiction, I'm high and feel great— but not because of him. Other times, when I'm in withdrawal, I'm despondent—again, not because of him. Since all my moods reflect this secret life he barely knows about, every day when he arrives home from work, he doesn't know—but also doesn't want to know—whom he will greet at the door. "She's always in that room," he says. "The house is a mess. She cries when she sees food. She hasn't worked in two years. I really think she'd feel better—what she *needs*—is to get out of the house, get a job, earn money. Be like other women."

Everything he says is true. I stare at the window, at a dim pulse of sun against closed blinds.

"How do you feel about this?" Ted asks me.

Hopeless, I think. "Hopeful," I say. "I'll try very hard to do things when I get home."

"And I want to have sex with my wife," Andrew says. While he sits erect wearing a jacket and tie, I slouch in wrinkled clothes. I want to sit healthy and strong, but the more he speaks, the more exhausted I am. "I'm sick of being celibate."

Andrew, how can I let you touch my body? If I let you close enough to love me, if I get too close to you, your warm hands might melt my cool surfaces. You might make my skin cry.

"She used to love having sex with me," he adds. Now he turns to me, accusing. "At least I thought so."

Before we were married, I think.

I first had sex with Andrew while married to someone else. At that time, I craved having sex with Andrew because sex with strangers is intense. To my addict, sex with strangers feels emotionally safer: after all, *all* they want is sex. No complicated relationship. After we married, Andrew was no longer a stranger; therefore, sex no longer felt safe. My addict wants a relationship with no history. My addict can't feel the intensity it craves with someone too familiar. Always drunk, it can't have sex sober.

"Do you want to give her another chance?" Ted asks.

"I guess so," Andrew says, sighing.

Now Ted asks me what I want to say to Andrew. I want to ask him to notice me. I want to tell him I don't want to be either his straying father or his weeping mother. I don't want to be an inanimate wife. Ted has told me I won't be inanimate if I am honest with Andrew about the addiction. He urges *me* to do this, for Ted, as my therapist, won't, can't, tell

Andrew about the men until I am ready. I *do* want to tell
Andrew the truth. But I'm ashamed—and afraid he'll hate
me, leave me—even though I would explain that without
those men, without the addiction, I could really love *him*.
That I don't love those other men.

"I wish, I guess I wish he—you—" I look at Andrew,
"weren't scared of me." Andrew stares past my head. He
shifts his weight and crosses his legs.

"Are you?" Ted asks Andrew.

"Well, most of the time she's a mess."

"Then you're scared something bad might happen to her?"
Ted asks.

"Of course I don't want anything bad to happen to her.
She's still my wife." He pauses. "But I'm tired of shouldering
all the responsibility. She could at least try to get a job teaching or something—after all that effort to get her MFA
degree. We'd starve to death if it weren't for me."

Except we *are* starving to death, I think. An insufficiency
of love.

"But what scares you?" Ted persists.

Andrew looks at me for one long moment. "Sometimes . . .
I guess I don't know who you are."

I walk with Andrew to the end of the hall, to the small sixth-
floor lobby. "Too bad Quizzle's not here," he says, nodding
toward the fish in the aquarium.

Quizzle, our cat. "Does she miss me?"

"She goes upstairs to your room and looks around. But
then she comes back down when she doesn't find you."

We have spent hours discussing Quizzle, worrying about her feelings—much safer than discussing our own.

Andrew, six feet tall, bends to hug me. Maybe because of his height, his hugs seem awkward. I don't know how to fit against his body. His shoulders brush mine. He brusquely pats my back, yes, the way he pats Quizzle. I do not know how to tell him I want something different. We do not kiss. Andrew straightens his tie and heads for the elevator. I do not call to him, do not ask him if he, too, goes upstairs to look for me, do not tell him I want him to, do not tell him I want him to find me.

I sit on the couch in front of the aquarium.

I don't really know who you are.

How *can* Andrew know who I am, when I wear the Janus mask of an addict?

In one phase of the addiction, like at parties, in order to hide insecurities and shyness, I'm boisterous—a boozy flirt. I am drunk, not on alcohol, but on men—so many men at this party. Should I flirt with you? Or you?

But when no man desires me or my body, I'm in withdrawal, what Andrew calls a "mess." I lie in bed weeping, anorexic, flipping from "acting out" to "acting in," from devouring everything in sight to refusing to nurture my body at all. For my eating addiction is faithful to this sex addiction. When I'm high and feel great, I eat. In sexual withdrawal, I starve because no body is needed.

So there's the addict dressed to seduce and dazzle; there's the addict in withdrawal. Yet there is also, at times, a small, sane voice that forces me to know something is wrong.

Vaguely, I recognize it is wrong to seduce a man when I'm engaged to be married, wrong to seduce a man scant weeks after being married. Then I try to set standards. I try to admit there *might* be a very small problem here. These times, I try to imitate what I consider normal behavior. I cook and clean. I am especially diligent on the job. I am quiet, proper, bland, calm.

But I'm not really sober. Because eventually, whether after four days or four years, this blandness makes me restless and edgy. How can I possibly fill up all that empty time? I create excuses to binge: it has rained every day for a week, or it's a holiday, or it's too hot, or there's a full moon, or my car has a flat tire, or my best friend lost her job, or there's a birthday to celebrate, or my boss is angry, or there's . . . always something.

And I find a man. And I'm right smack back where I began in this cycle of addiction.

Of course, being an addict, terrified of intimacy, it never occurs to me (even *after* I achieve some awareness) to explain or confess these fears, this information, to Andrew. Never. So how can he know me? How can I know him, either?

To me, his desire for the ordinary is an exotic, unyielding mystery. Although when I *am* in that relatively sober state, I *do* help peel wallpaper and paint the walls in the living room. Weed the garden. Make sure birds have sunflower seeds in the feeder. The oil in the cars is changed every three thousand miles. Tires are rotated. Clothes are laundered on Sunday. Shirts are ironed, and food is cooked for dinner.

Socks are matched and neatly rolled, underwear folded and placed in the proper dresser drawer. We insulate the attic and lay a new rug in the bathroom. We remodel the kitchen.

But we both know that even when I do ordinary things, my heart isn't in it. Ultimately my mind drifts, and I don't know how to reel it back long enough to save coupons or make grocery lists. I stand in the vegetable aisle of Kroger crying, surrounded by so much food, uncertain what to buy. I return from Kroger with six or seven sacks—but nothing in those sacks resembles food that could be transformed into a nourishing meal. I can barely even arrange the superficially perfect image—like Shirley, like my mother—of a fake happy family eating dinner.

Why does he stay with me? Why not leave? Does he stay because he pities me? Because he thinks I'd crash-land without him? Why doesn't he see what he sees? Why doesn't he know what he knows? Why doesn't he see the outrageously sexual clothes I buy to appease my addict? Why doesn't he see I never wear these clothes for him? Why doesn't he see me the days I return home smelling like the Rainbow Motel? Why does he never notice?

Why do I stay with him? Because I *want* to want what he wants. I want to want the exotic ordinary.

I'm here in the hospital because I believe therapy will conjure me into that kind of woman.

So far it hasn't. As long as I crave Gabriel/Rick, it won't.

I float between worlds. I can't firmly plant my feet in Andrew's real earth because I'm scared they'll root forever.

But I'm also unable to survive in Rick/Gabriel's world because the air is too thin and no one remembers to eat dinner.

Andrew, you are a ghost husband. How can I see you—a vague spirit drifting along hallways of our deserted marriage?

Linda comes in and sits beside me on the couch across from the aquarium. "I saw you and your husband leave Ted's office," she says.

"I don't think we're getting anywhere."

"*Husbands.* Mine thinks I'm a terrible person. A slut."

"But you're *not*," I say.

"Except you wouldn't believe some of the awful things I've done." She tells me that once, on a vacation to St. Simons Island with her husband and kids, she had her lover drive down and check into another motel room. And she went back and forth between the two rooms for the entire trip.

"But we've *all* done bad stuff." I tell her about the obscene phone caller. I tell her about another man, also in Boston, who parked for hours beside my dorm in a red Corvette. "I thought that was so cool, that he would do that," I say. "And one day I just drove off with him, even though I was having an affair with a married man at the same time."

"Would you let me read your Workbook when you finish writing your history?" Linda asks.

This is part of the recovery. We're each to choose a partner and let her read the First Step in our Workbook. This will lessen the shame we feel about our behaviors.

I'd wanted Jill for a partner. Except Jill would romanticize all the things I've done with men. Get high off it.

"Yes," I say to Linda.

WORKBOOK—FIRST STEP FOR ADDICTS

Forrest and the obscene phone caller aren't the only dangerous men I meet in Boston. That autumn when I watch Forrest from my window, I watch another man, too. Bored waiting for three o'clock, for Forrest to cross the street bouncing his basketball, I open my bay window, lean out, and see a man parked in his red Corvette directly below. He sits in his car for hours—much more dependable than Forrest—just to catch a glimpse of me, I believe, even as I suspect he waits for any body.

Soon it is not enough only to watch him from my window. Returning from class one Monday, I walk past the car scuffing my loafers through autumn leaves. The drawstring of my green bookbag is wrapped around my palm, the bag dangling by my leg. I look at him as I pass the car; then I glance back over my shoulder. I repeat this ritual on Tuesday, Wednesday, Thursday. On Friday I smile and walk over. On Friday I grip my bookbag against my chest when he rolls down the window.

He wears a black leather jacket and smokes a cigarette. I ask why he sits here so many hours. "Maybe I'm watching you," he says.

I nod, then walk inside the dorm. For now, knowing he watches me is enough to make me feel strong and powerful.

Away from Boston over Christmas, I stare out my bedroom window as if it replicates the dorm window—imagining not only Forrest, but also this other man, and I will know, by looking at my suburban yard in New Jersey, that the man in Boston still waits. In the reality of this magic, yes, I see him and know, since he's waited so long to meet me, this must be love. He has not grown bored while I'm away. Nor will he have a suspicious wife. He will be faithful.

So my first day back I am not surprised that red metal is the only color I see in the gray-white cold of January. The swirl of snow obliterates even the brick of Back Bay, while his car, a beacon, beckons. I barely consider Forrest at this moment. I don't care if he sees me. How can he even notice me? For although I'm drunk on the sight of red metal, I feel sober enough to slip past radar undetected.

Before I grasp the handle I know the door will be unlocked. I know it's always been unlocked, waiting for me. Without asking I open the passenger door. Without asking I sink onto the seat, my legs weak, indelible with longing. Carelessly, I dump my bookbag on the floor and smile.

Inside his car, now finally inside, I can't see out. Behind a veil of snow Boston is vague, effaced, is "out there." While I am "in here." Only this man inside the car, this man who smells of Aqua Velva and black leather, exists. He rubs his hand along my arm, my brown suede jacket. He asks where I want to go. Do I need a ride? I need—I say I want to know his name. That I've come here. *This* is where I'm going. He says he'll tell me his name if I'll come with him now. I don't ask where. I know where we are going.

He drives toward the harbor and stops before a run-down building. He yanks the emergency brake and gets out, knowing I'll follow. I follow him upstairs to a second-floor apartment. I have no desire to flee. I have to do this. I want to. This is why I watched him all autumn into winter. Yes, yes, there is fear, but I am drawn to it, crave it, have driven on slick streets in a car of dangerous red metal just to feel it.

He slams the door behind us. I think he slams it, but maybe it is my heart slamming. He bolts the lock, slips on a chain. My bookbag tumbles to the floor. The room is ice-cold and my arms break out in a sweat. He turns on a gas space heater. A small whoosh of flame startles the brown shag carpet littered with lint, startles the ripped window shades, the plastic sofa.

He kneels on the floor before me, unzips my jacket, and presses his head against my stomach. He slides his hand up past my blue knee socks, my bare thighs, and touches my underpants. The tips of his fingers slip underneath—the cold startles me—and I think he warms them on me. I want him to. I know I can warm them.

He says he bets this suburban girl has never let anyone touch her there before. I whisper this is true, nodding my head, my lie sounding real—because *I believe*, in this one drunk moment, I have never felt sheer blue ice melt my skin before. He asks if I want him to touch me there, what do I want, "tell me." And all I can say is yes, I want him to do this, yes.

He pulls me toward the bedroom. I have trouble walking. He lifts me. An iron barbell is on the floor in front of a full-length mirror. A white jock strap hangs on the knob of the door leading to the bathroom. He holds me over the bed and opens his arms. It seems to take forever for my body to drain down to the mattress. He crashes beside me. My body feels jolted by love. My tongue, when he kisses me, touches his teeth and feels as if it presses freezing metal. There is a large black birthmark on the side of his neck that seeps beneath his hairline. I touch it. The skin is rough. He punches my arm and pins it against the bed and tells me never to touch it again. His eyes are cold and blue, and all I feel while he is doing this—*this*—is the touch of his black birthmark on my finger.

I know it is a sign of dark magic revealing secrets of all the nights of my past as well as my future.

In class the next day, how carefully I reconstruct my mask of a college student. In sweater, miniskirt, loafers, I sit at my desk and appear to concentrate on writing an English essay. I want to do well. I want to get an A on the essay. We are assigned a comparison/contrast essay and given a list of possible subjects.

None interest me. Can I compare the girl of today with the girl of yesterday?

Am I having trouble selecting a subject? my English teacher asks. "Write about something you're familiar with," she suggests. "Something you know about."

You don't want to know what I know. I didn't even know

what I knew. Back then, I didn't know why I craved those men. I needed them because I had always needed them, ever since I could remember.

I don't know how to write the essay.

"Why don't you try comparing high school with college?" she says. "Or contrast the two. What're the differences?"

There is nothing to contrast. There are no differences. I received terrible grades in high school. I'm scared I'll fail here. I'm scared I'll receive an F on this essay. Truly, there are too many similarities.

My English teacher sits beside me. "Maybe you're not ready to write a comparison essay," she says. "Would you rather write a descriptive essay? You could write about your dorm room."

I know this essay should not be complicated, but my mind feels dazed by the man in the Corvette. If only I could write a description of him, of his room, describe how I'm able to open the door to his car and drive off with this man I have always known . . . to a room I always enter . . . how I drive with that man back to the Ritz-Carlton . . . farther, miles and years backward . . . swerving out of the way of love to reach one of the bedrooms I shared with my father.

Except, even in college, I didn't know how to explain about that room when I was in second grade, with windows up near the ceiling, too high for anyone to see in, to know what my father and I were doing. Only my father knew how to track me through doors and windows, brick and plaster. And when he found me I felt as if my true self vanished, swallowed by his thirsty night. By morning, all that seemed to remain of either of us was a smudge on once-white sheets, and a vague fear it would be impossible to clean them.

Back then, I didn't know how to explain that thirst, that room, that father, those nights.

Nor did I know how to explain about the room I entered yesterday.

"Just try the dorm," the teacher urges.

My dorm room has tan walls with pieces of Scotch tape and thumbtack holes where girls have hung posters and pictures. I bought a red paisley bedspread and matching curtains at Filene's Basement. The other girls on the hall are energetic, always rushing off to school activities. They also study a lot and get good grades.

I wonder if, back in my dorm, the phone might be ringing. I imagine it is. It could be the obscene phone caller. It could be the man in the Corvette, even though he doesn't know my name or my number. It could be Forrest, telling me his wife is no longer suspicious. It doesn't matter which man. They all want sex as much as I want them to want it. It doesn't matter where it happens. The essence of all the rooms is the same.

The girls in the next room have a record player and they play Johnny Mathis records at night. I hear his voice through the thin wall. It helps me sleep. The dorm is a red brick building in Back Bay and my room has a bay window. When I look out the window and down at the street I see a man sitting in a car, in a red Corvette.

I cross out the last sentence.

I get a C+ on the essay. "No spelling or grammar errors. But not very original. Put more of yourself into the essay."

Who?

I have no language to describe either part of me. It is not unfamiliarity with the word *addiction*; it is unfamiliarity with the word *me*. I have no language to think of myself in disparate pieces. I have no language to explain.

I receive a D on a multiple-choice psychology exam. My professor wants to see me. I knew I did poorly even before the test was returned. How can I choose one correct answer when so many are possible? I know, for example, it is possible to appear to be one kind of girl yet act as if I'm another kind altogether, possible to smile shyly and speak politely to teachers while thinking about fucking men who drive red Corvettes.

"Is anything wrong?" my psychology teacher asks when I sit in his office.

I shake my head. "No," I say. "Nothing's wrong."

There is a black and white photograph of a woman on the corner of his desk. I look at his left hand. He wears a wedding ring. To me, of course, this is not an obstacle if I want to seduce him. If I seduce him maybe I'll get a better grade. Maybe he wants me to. Maybe this is why he invited me to meet with him in his office.

"You sure?" His hair is strawberry blond and thinning, his eyes gentle. "If there's anything at all to talk about . . ."

No one has ever asked me if something is wrong, or if there is anything to talk about. So how would I even know if something is wrong? How could I answer?

Through the window pale winter sun slants across his desk. I want to bend forward, rest my head in the sunlight, and sleep. "No, really," I say.

Besides, you, gentle man with the wedding ring, are too delicate to listen to stories about men who make obscene phone calls. How could *you* understand the touch of that birthmark on my fingertip, the mark of the man in the Corvette?

I know this.

Even as I know that you, man with the wedding ring, only want to help me and do not want me to seduce you, do not want me for sex.

Again, he asks if he can help me with a problem. "Or come back some other time," he urges. "Anytime you feel like talking, okay?"

I can't answer. I don't know how to speak to men who don't want sex with me. Nor do I know if I have a problem. Am *I* a problem? Are there right answers and wrong answers? Good choices and bad choices? Maybe I need his multiple-choice exam sheet with all the answers, the key.

Never do I feel as if I belong in college. I can't concentrate on classes. I can't understand their importance. Nor do I belong with the girls in the dorm, girls who don't drive off with men in red Corvettes.

So on snowy winter nights I escape dorms and books and college and sit in the Hayes-Bickford Cafeteria near Copley

Square. I buy a cup of tea and watch ancient, homeless men sipping cold coffee. Their clothes, creased with dirt, are the color of mud and rain. Their hands shake. Their bodies are frail and deficient. They smell of blight and of the hour just before dawn. Patchy whiskers stubble wind-chapped faces. They sit alone at tables staring into coffee cups or out ice-glazed windows, their eyes gluey with age, as if searching for the contents of their lives.

I come here because I want to be one of these men, spend evenings in the Hayes-Bickford, a homeless blur. I am this blur. Homeless. Why not? Dangerous men know my phone number and know in which dorm room I sleep.

The next day Forrest calls and says he saw me drive off with a man in a red Corvette.

Yes, I say. This is what I have done.

He is the one to call me Slut.

Because I am.

DAY
ELEVEN

As our group walks up the path to the High Museum of Art, past the Calder sculpture, I watch my once-red shoelaces, grayed with dust (which I still haven't tied since arriving on the unit—I have no idea why), trail through puddles from last night's rain. I drift to the rear. Gabriel, who drove us, leads the way, a white feather in the rubber band securing his braid. Jill laughs at something he says, but I am distant from the sound, distant from all these people, even Gabriel. The shame I feel that I waited outside to meet him that night, and knowing I would wait again—that I lied about it to Ted, and would lie again—*this* shame—feels like a rock, heavy in my mouth. If I open my mouth, the other women, everyone, will see it.

The air is still. It is September, not cool, not warm, no defining character. The seasons, time, seem changeless. Like me. I feel trapped in cells that won't shed or regenerate. I am no different from the girl raised by my father, no different from the college student who met Forrest at the Ritz-Carlton. Then, too, I was afraid to speak to the girls in my dorm, scared to be noticed, scared they'd see shame creasing my skin. So I've never really changed, nothing has changed at all.

I sit on a bench in one of the galleries. Before me is a ghostly painting of a river and gothic buildings misted in fog. A dreamlike sun obscures more than illuminates: buildings, water, sun evanesce with the stroke of a brush. The painting is flat, dead, the images distant, hung on a white wall in an airless room. In the strict parameters of its frame, the painting is like my life: boundaried by frames I don't know how to break.

I imagine the painting unhooking itself from the wall, becoming life. The frame crashes to the floor. Without its rigid boundary, I am washed in quivering light, breathing earth, water, air, drenched in luminous impressions.

I feel a presence behind me. I blink.

The glimpse is ephemeral. The painting is back in the frame, rehung on the wall.

This presence . . .

I do not turn around. I know who he is and why he has

come. "Sorry 'bout the other night," he says. "At the last minute I thought, if we met, you might have second thoughts after and tell Ted."

"I'd never tell him." I grip the edge of the bench. I feel him just behind me. I know if I move my head the tiniest bit I will touch him. "I *want* to see you."

With a finger, he traces my bare shoulder along the ripped seam of my T-shirt. He slips his hand under the shirt and presses his palm against my collarbone. The cool silver of his necklace touches my cheek. His hair smells of jasmine incense.

"Want to meet you, too." There's so much we can learn about love, he tells me. About the silence of love. About knowing how to show it without words—just listening to the other's body.

"That sounds . . . almost spiritual," I say.

"It's *very* spiritual."

"You've loved a lot of women like that."

"I love all women like that."

Then you can love me like that, I think. I want to taste tobacco-colored skin. I want to feel caressed in a blizzard of white feathers. All I care about is escaping my consciousness. Entering his.

Against the back of my head I feel pressure. He leans over and whispers, "I promise I'll meet you in the lounge later."

I glance up at him. I believe him because I must.

He removes a piece of paper from his pocket. A note, he says, to read later. It, too, smells of jasmine. I clasp it in my hand, my fingertips reading the braille of his secret message. A rush of liquid air gusts across my heart. Like windburn. Like love.

Gabriel is moving away. White feather. Turquoise earring. Silver beads. Scar on his arm. Without looking back at me, he walks to the entrance of the gallery. Jill stands there, watching him. She smiles at him as he passes.

After ten P.M., and I can't find Gabriel. The lounge is deserted. The remainder of the evening stretches endlessly, and I don't know what to do. I must find Gabriel. I must find him NOW. I don't know how to fill time on my own. Always, in the addiction, I need a thing, an object, a prop, a crutch, *another* addiction, to carry me forward from this specific moment into the next, and the next . . . until all common sense has been erased.

I cross the hall to one of the empty rooms. I sit on the bed and stare at the telephone. I feel as if I must find him, own him, possess him: immediately. I want to call him at home. I can't call him at home. Suppose he doesn't answer. Suppose he does answer, but when he hears my voice he slams down the phone. Suppose I've said or done something that's caused him to hate me. Suppose a woman answers.

I pick up the receiver. I'm grateful I don't know his number. I can't ask the operator for it. She will know why I want it, will know why I want *him*. Or his number might not be listed. And I will know, for sure, I'll never see him again.

I dial Ted's voice mail. If I can focus on one thing that's

real. One person. Mainline reality. Although I know virtually nothing of Ted's personal life, still, he is more knowable, more real, than Gabriel.

"Hi. You have reached Ted's confidential voice mail. At the sound of the tone you will have two minutes to leave your name, your number, and a message, and I'll return your call as soon as I'm available. Thank you."

I hang up and redial. I must hear Ted's voice again. "Hi. You have reached . . ."

"Ted," I whisper after the tone.

I press the receiver to my neck as if he can hear what I should say. I want to apologize for the way I acted the other day when he came to my room in his ripped jeans and T-shirt. I want to say the word *help* into the receiver. But I don't know how to tell Ted I'm in trouble.

Nor can I say the name *Gabriel* to Ted. Gabriel will be fired. He will hate me forever. I'll never see him again. I let the tape on the machine run its two minutes while concentrating on the word *Gabriel* as if Ted, when he checks his messages, will be able to read my mind on the silent tape and know how to help me.

Ted can't read minds. I hang up the phone.

I need Gabriel, a man who's as soothing as vodka, as dangerous as sexual roulette. If not him, I need drugs, pills, Xanax, scotch, sex, love, suicide, starvation, all the chocolate in the southeastern United States. Unconsciousness. I don't know how to get through the night without Gabriel. Worse, I don't know how to get through the next thirty seconds. The next second seems like an eternity. I need a fix. A balm.

Something to soothe me. Anything that might mimic Gabriel. Only with Gabriel will the slow crawl of real time propel me into the quick heat of addiction. Only with Gabriel can I interrupt time, dissolve space. Until there is no me on the rehab unit. Until there is no unit.

From my pocket, I remove the piece of paper Gabriel gave me at the museum: *The only infallible, immutable, unlimited power that heals, without question, is love.*

But does he love me? Where is he if he loves me? Why didn't he meet me when he promised?

Love. My father told me he loved me. So did that writer of fictions. I must make myself understand that Gabriel's love is the same as that writer's. I must make myself project into the future to know that *if* I pursue Gabriel, then what happened with the writer could also happen with Gabriel. I must understand that, potentially, there is no difference between the two.

I meet that haggard, hungover writer at a conference. I am coming off a long binge, so I first refuse sex with him, even though I flirt outrageously. And he must hear this refusal as a challenge. Up the ante from affair to marriage, he must calculate, promising he'll leave his wife, I should leave Andrew and move in with him. It's not that I actually believe him; when I feel the true intent of his offer pierce me with the slender gentleness of a hypodermic needle, I don't. Rather, it is my addictwoman who believes him: both she and he elide truth. *She* accepts this idea of a perfect marriage: dangerous sex, year after year, with one dangerous man. No need to waste time cruising the hot breath of night searching for a fix, when a live-in fix is ready and waiting.

We will meet again in a month, he says, where he'll be giving a reading in Iowa. I have a month to consider the offer, consider sex—but why not have sex, if we're to marry anyway?

For a month, day after day in my house in Georgia, I lie in bed, barely moving, thinking I am in love, that this luxurious state of emotional chaos is love. I tell myself I'll feel better when he and I are together, that it is the missing of him that causes fatigue, even though I must know this is a lie.

Rather, it is the anticipation of him that causes my body, preparing to be throttled, to enter a state of decrement. I eat one carrot stick in the morning and another for dinner. I chew slowly, my teeth feeling softer than mush. My eyes stare at dust, at what I am becoming. All I hear is my heart beating in my stomach as it tries to digest this huge sludge of shredded carrot.

When I am not nibbling carrot sticks I am weeping, sleepless nights, weeping—because, really, I *don't* want to leave Andrew. I don't want to meet the writer in one month. In that small second-story bedroom, in that twin bed above Andrew's bedroom, my blood thins to tears. I think all that liquid will seep through floorboards, drain down walls, and dampen the sheets and pillow upon which Andrew sleeps. I want him to cup his palms and contain my liquescent body. I want him to soothe my emaciated frame. I want him to stop me from meeting the writer. I want him to help me. Protect me.

I want the impossible. For what I *really* want, have always needed, is a mother to sit beside me, a daughter on her sickbed, and press a damp washcloth to my forehead. I need a mother to guard the threshold of her daughter's bedroom, lock the door, hide the key. It is a mother whom I want to protect me, a mother to teach me how to protect myself.

In disgust at my weeping, the semester over, Andrew leaves for California. He leaves me too free, too light, no more tears to weight my body in the house.

Yes, Andrew, go, I think. Leave. Why bother staying? After all, there is no fence, guardrail, blockade solid enough to prevent that writer from slicing through the bone and tissue of your wife. He is a fusillade of lust splintering our door.

I fly to Iowa to meet the writer. The plane misses its first attempt at landing. Through dull and faded eyes I see the runway rush up toward the wheels . . . then grow dimmer in my field of vision as the plane veers almost straight up. My heart does not pound. My knees do not weaken. Again, as when the men with the knife stopped me in Boston, I don't know how to register fear and am unable to distinguish between my self and a potential plane crash.

How surprised Andrew will be when he learns I have died in a plane crash in Iowa, I think calmly. He does not know I am here. He does not know I have gone out of town for the weekend. He thinks I am home in Georgia.

The plane does not crash, of course.

I do. One long weekend crash.

Yet a crash that is silent.

I am in bed with that writer of fiction in a motel room. He does not notice I am skinny. I do not tell him I am down to two carrot sticks a day. He does not notice I am skeletal bones with a small mound of stomach. We have come here to feed off each other, fatten each other up. Drink this sweat, I think, even as I know he drinks the sediment of my heart. In this motel room we subsist on gruel drier than dust. We breathe hermetic air. I am down to ninety pounds, exfoliated to a nub. Still, we will gnaw on each other, eat each other up.

This weekend, this protean man is no longer romance and false promises. The marriage proposal dries in his smoky mouth. He speaks career sex as if it's business language. No tasty metaphors or euphemisms. The word *love* does not enter the picture or wear feathered masks.

Wait.

There is a mask. Its mouth is desperate, famished, enraged: the face of my father.

Lying in bed beside him, I hear summer crack into jagged sheets of heat. I don't know how to get home in one piece. I imagine this motel room lifting right up off its foundation and whirling down the street, blasting across state lines and crashing into an arid dimension of space. All that will be left of either of us is a stain across an anonymous carpet.

Returning home on the plane, I am too dazed to locate my assigned seat. I drain into the first empty seat I find. The man in whose seat I mistakenly sit takes one look at me and finds another seat, without saying a word.

DAY
TWELVE

WHEN I WAKE it is close to dawn. Jill is not in the room. I know where she is. At this moment, now, I *must* make myself know what I know.

I must leave here. Now. I can't wait.

I can't wait for her to return trailing jasmine incense, her hair decorated with white feathers. She will carry the musk of danger in her pockets.

Ted has told me to be safe. This unit isn't. The danger is *here*, not out there. Outside *must* be safer.

I wash and pull on a pair of black denims, a T-shirt and sweatshirt, socks, red Reeboks, still not tying the laces. I pick up my keys and wallet and leave the door wide open to wel-

come Jill when she returns home from her blissfully dangerous journey.

I slip from the unit. I move slowly. Without Gabriel—or
some man—shading my body, I believe I am invisible, so
why hurry? I move as if I'm sleepwalking, lighter than air.
The elevator rushing me to the lobby barely registers my
presence. I see rain, yet I slowly cross the parking lot, not
sure if rain touches me. How can it if I'm no longer visible?
I unlock my car door, almost surprised the key works, surprised the car still exists, for I haven't touched it in almost
two weeks. I sit behind the steering wheel, run a finger
around the rim. This, at least, is tangible. This blue steering
wheel exists.

I turn from the lot onto the parkway. I switch on the
lights, the windshield wipers, the heater. I shift when I
should. I wonder whether I made a mistake not to have
brought my suitcase. But it's too late to go back.

When I stop at a traffic light I glance to my right, almost
expecting to see Jim, that man from the 12-Step group, still
waiting for the girl in her Camaro. I want to see him—knowing I could easily convince him that my blue Honda is a red
Camaro. A man in a suit drums his hand against the steering
wheel of a tan Chevy as if in time to music. Another man.
Another Jim. I think about getting out of my car. Rapping on
his window. I could tell him to skip work and come with me,
that I could bring him a lifetime of pleasure in one hour in
room #213 of the Rainbow Motel. The light turns green. He
drives away.

Inside the Krispy Kreme Donut Shoppe, I sit on a plastic stool. The plate-glass windows are silver with raindrops. Headlights, taillights scud wet pavement. Fluorescent lights harden the counter. There are no shadows. I order one glazed doughnut. An elderly woman sits beside me and orders two Krispy Kreme doughnuts. Her stockings wrinkle about her ankles. Two teenagers explode through the door. The girl wears a gold-plated bracelet that's tarnished another bracelet onto the skin of her wrist. Her boyfriend gives her fleeting, wispy kisses. I kick off my Reeboks and yank off my wet socks, leaving the socks on the floor. I put my shoes back on, pick up the doughnut, and walk outside. I get in my car and drive from the lot. Checking for traffic, I catch a glimpse of myself in the rearview mirror. And now, even though the car moves forward, I feel as if I could let the mirror literally pull me back in time . . . back to Gabriel, back to the Rainbow Motel, back to the Ritz-Carlton. Back to those seedy bars in Galveston when I felt STRANDED ON THE STRAND, married to my first husband. Back.

On the loop, rain ebbs to a drizzle. I'm in the slow lane driving as if I'm arthritic and traffic swishes past. I slump low in the seat and think about never leaving my car, even sleeping here. Enveloped in the car's hum, I believe all voices can be silenced. Keep driving. I can go anywhere in my mind—travel on endless highways or toward impossible destinations. Yes, I can journey back to homeless men who sip cold coffee from chipped mugs in the Hayes-Bickford in Boston. I sit beside them and eat Krispy Kreme doughnuts, our callused elbows resting on Formica tables.

As the drizzly mist lifts, a thin sun dries the clouds. I turn off the heater. With the deepening sun I feel panic rising. Gray feels safer. Rain feels safer. Anything feels safer than sun. I want Gabriel, his dark hair and skin, to protect me from the glare.

I stop at a Hungry Harvey for gasoline, edging the car next to a pump. I depress the lever to fill the tank. Along the loop people rush to work, rush toward definite locations I don't understand.

This is what I understand: in the next bay a man in a turtleneck with a heavy gold chain around his neck pumps gas into a BMW. He wears sunglasses, but still I know he watches me. I stare at him, too—cool, smug, distant—see how far he'll go with this, betting I can go further.

I wait in line to pay the cashier. I sense the man behind me, closer than necessary. On the counter is a small tub of rosebuds, a display of chewing tobacco, candy, gum. I hand the cashier my Visa and lean against the counter. The man edges forward and places his elbow next to mine. Barely, he presses my arm. If I'm who he thinks I am, he does this on purpose; if I'm not, he can pretend it's a mistake. I'm racing with possibilities. Racing across the country in a BMW. Riding elevators into a high-rise condo with white walls and black sheets. His black velvet bedspread is reflected in the mirror over his bed. As I turn to leave I smile at him, hard . . . but continue out the door.

The Coke-bottle-green-tiled bathroom of the Hungry Harvey is dim, windowless. No sounds seep in from outside. I lean my hands on the counter and close my eyes. I am weightless. Disconnecting too quickly from the unit, from Ted, rising up, up, up into real time too fast. For the first time in weeks no one knows where I am. The sudden freedom is relentless. I must slow down.

I must stop this.

I open my eyes and look at myself in the mirror. Call someone. Anyone. Even connecting with my own image in the mirror is better than nothing. But in this green wavery light I don't know if I see my self or my addict. I must call Ted. I've made a mistake, but I can go back.

I go to the pay phone at the edge of the parking lot. Scratched into the metal box is the message: "Call 309-6090 4XTC2NITE." I drop a quarter in the slot. I listen to the dial tone. But that dial tone. All the numbers. Too many possibilities. Too many men, too many choices. I wonder if 309-6090 is a man. I'm floundering, my hands cold with sweat. I look around the lot, half expecting to see a message, as if the pole holding the Hungry Harvey logo will suddenly be transfigured into a sign to show me the way. Rain begins again. Wind gusts candy wrappers and dead leaves against the pay phone. Plastic flags strung across the lot smack the breeze.

Ted, I don't know how to call you. I don't have a message for your voice mail.

I call Rick and drive around until I find a cash machine for First Union bank.

I reach the Rainbow Motel before he does. No longer does the motel owner, the father of the little girl, ask me to register. Rick and I are known here, are good customers. I place

$29.95 on the counter. I am given the key—yes, room #213—like always. The young daughter sits on the linoleum floor of the lobby playing with a Barbie doll. She wears jeans and a cotton shirt, the collar starched and unwrinkled. I want to ask the girl her name, but I don't want her to see me.

I shut the door to #213 but don't lock it. The familiarity of the room soothes. The smell of chlorine. Damp sheets. Plastic curtains. I turn on the light next to the bed. I shiver. Today is the first time since last spring we won't need the air conditioner. I step from my Reeboks and pull off my damp denims and sweatshirt. In the bathroom I turn on the shower, the spray hot as I can stand it. As water washes over me, I feel as if my skin is dissolving. I want it to. I want to be steam dispersing to air. I want to see Rick as much as I dread it. I want him to transport me as far away from Gabriel as possible.

The outside knob turns. The door slams shut. I hear the bolt. The chain. Footsteps pad threadbare carpet. Rick stands outside the shower. A cigarette is clamped between his lips. He inhales before balancing the cigarette on the edge of the sink. He unbuttons his shirt and drops it on the floor. Blond hair. Gold necklace. He kicks off his loafers. I hear a zipper. The rustle of material. We do not speak or greet each other. His cool eyes watch me—no—they watch a body. He steps into the shower behind me. He grips his arms around my waist and pushes me slightly forward. I must press my palms against the tiles for balance. The fuck is brief. For a moment, after, he still holds me; when he releases me I slowly sink to the floor of the tub. He turns off the water.

"I wish we could spend the day together," he says. "But I've got a meeting." He dresses and relights the cigarette. "At least we had time to do what was important." He bends to kiss me good-bye.

I lean back in the tub. Water from the nozzle drips onto my right foot. I think I hear an alarm. I am shivering, my hair wet, my body damp. Stiffly, I return to the bedroom. On the dresser next to the television is Rick's fifteen dollars, half the price of the fuck.

I wrap the green bedspread around me, over my head, and sit cross-legged on the bed. I don't know how to leave this familiar place for one that's different. All I ever seem to do is retrace my footsteps, over and over, always ending up *here*, in all the room #213s, in all the Rainbow Motels. In this sick, sick, sickness I believe I have betrayed Gabriel, not my husband. In this sickness, I believe I love Gabriel. This competition, the relationship of me/Jill/Gabriel, seems especially familiar.

It is familiar because there's always been three, at least three people, in every relationship I've had.

Me, Jill, Gabriel.

Me, Rick, his wife.

Me, my husband, another man. And *that* man's wife, as well—if there is one.

Me, my father, my mother.

Yet even with all these people, I have always felt alone. I even felt alone at the wedding party for my first marriage. I remember watching my new husband dance with other women, the guests. I have no recollection of dancing with

him myself. I sat at a table during the party in a navy blue
dress I'd bought at a boutique in Georgetown, my face
splotched with hives—I'd broken out just that morning. I
was confused as to what to expect from marriage. I was
uncertain if I had the right to ask my own husband to dance.
Did I have to wait for him to notice me? I didn't understand
the word *husband*. Or the word *wife*.

Yet I married this man—just as I later married Andrew—
because of a vague sense I need a husband to *save* me from
this clutter of other relationships, other people, other men.
Because I trusted non sequiturs, false analogies, false causes, I
believed that the state of marriage would, by definition,
reconfigure me into a sober, proper woman and wife. I
believed that the state of being faithful was an element
inherent to the state of matrimony. Therefore, I would no
longer be a slut.

I also married simply because this man was the first to ask
me. I was overcome by the honor of becoming a man's wife.
Besides, with one constant man, surely I would no longer be
lonely.

After our wedding, we leave Washington and move to
Galveston for my husband's new job. That first month, the
hives on my face spread to my body, for I realize I have not
learned how to conjugate the verb *married* into behavior.
The more distant I grow from my workaholic husband, the
more I believe I need a man, then another man, to fill the
expanding emptiness I feel. Similarly, as I abandon my true

self (and become my addict self) when I act out with these men, I mistakenly believe I need more and more men in order *not* to feel abandoned or lonely. *They* must be the answer. Month after month, the addiction escalates. Married, my behaviors become more destructive—not less.

My husband travels, and I watch for him to leave town as if he's a semaphore. With the coast clear, I slip from my daybody, don my nightbody, and journey into moonblind nights. Neon lights on bars by the wharves flicker and hum. The Caine Mutiny. The Kon Tiki. The Moulin Rouge. Bars are lavish with laughter, smoke, drunken stares, tense skin, seductive faces. A girl with a crimson scarf around her neck flirts with a man wearing a western shirt with rhinestone buttons. *I* can be this girl adorned with crimson scarves flirting with rhinestone cowboys.

I am this girl.

I drink scotch, straight. I set a glass stenciled with my lipstick on a pinball machine. I play, but it's pretense for my body leaning against the machine waiting to be noticed. The punch of the jukebox stuns the wood floor. Western boots, biker boots, punctuate each note. Music is incurable country-western. I dance all by myself, believing Glen Campbell recorded the song "Galveston" just for me. Smoke circles fanlights before catching in blades and spinning across the ceiling. I finish a scotch and ask for a tequila sunrise. But I am drunk way before the drinks.

Or I dance with bikers. Sailors off ships. Rednecks. I dance with anyone who asks, a biker in dirty jeans and Harley T-shirt. His arms envelope me, his hands at the base of my spine. My arms encircle his neck. As my shirt hikes up, he slides his hands beneath it. We don't speak. We don't need to.

Later, I watch topless dancers on a small raised stage, silvery bangles dangling from elbows to wrists. Black bikini pants and pasties with tassels. Blue and red lights flash. I watch a man watch the dancers, a cigarette suspended, forgotten for a moment between his fingers. I wish he watched me.

Mornings, regardless of nights filled with secrets, I show up for work. On time. In business clothes. I'm friendly and industrious. Seemingly sober and normal. I work hard all day, get the job done. So at my most self-destructive, I still try to preserve myself—even as the job means nothing. For, really, it is my secret world—obsessive, fully realized, detailed— that, ironically, saves me, that keeps me going through days that are vague and boring. I live the day world only because I know night is coming.

The moon glides into focus with the slow pulse of blues. Flowers are pinned in my hair. Gold-plated beads and dime-store earrings are fastened. Maybe once, glancing at my face in the mirror, I remember blue popit beads my father once bought as payment . . . the way he trailed blue beads across that naked, little-girl body. Quickly, quickly, I glance away, until these thoughts are blank spaces.

Neon nights, I walk the seawall. Harleys, Yamahas, Kawasakis roar down the strip. Trans-ams idle next to girls in cutoff jeans. I pass the Seahorse, the Flagship motels. Men stumble from bars. Others drift in, pausing to shine the tops of their boots on the calves of their jeans. I am tugged by the tidal undertow of men from one bar to the next, one man to the next—even though I know there will never be enough night-time to consume all the sin I'm after.

. . . But the next night you wouldn't know me. The next night, with my husband home, we eat at an expensive restaurant with his clients. My clothes are adult, my jewelry understated, my speech intelligent, I am a just-the-right-amount charming impostor. Dangerous cinnabar perfume dims to Chanel No. 5. I am vaguely bored. What makes the evening tolerable is knowing that no one knows me. What makes the evening tolerable is my belief in my power to per-mutate: the men from the night before wouldn't recognize me tonight; these well-to-do businesspeople wouldn't recog-nize me in a smoky bar with the small of my back pressed against a pinball machine. I am palatable in any setting.

When my husband is out of town, I cruise relentlessly. Once, on a whim, or because it's my birthday and he prom-ises, moreover, to love me forever, I run away from home with a man driving a blue Chevy convertible, top down. The sweaty sun hemorrhages across the Gulf, KILE on the radio, disco then, but it takes so little to feel voluptuous, "Stayin' Alive" (barely), racing across the San Louis Pass, circling the necklace of the Gulf Coast, distant towns lit like radioactive dust. We drive blind drunk on sex, cruising vertigo on hori-zontal highways.

Blue convertible and I make it to Matagorda. For two days clothes are strewn around a motel room like evidence. But the relationship crash-lands in the middle of nowhere on the way back.

After returning to Galveston, he "abandons" me for his wife. And I, exhausted, have nowhere to go but home. I skulk back to my apartment, arriving scant moments before my husband, who had, thankfully, been in Austin on business for the weekend.

Shamed and sober, I try to be one of those housewives who are intimate with supermarkets and laundry. This woman who strives to be a wife, wants to obliterate that addictgirl— the girl who knows how to run away from home more than she knows how to stay there. The girl who's great at beginnings. Endings are a sure bet for her, too. But it's the long sober tedium of the middle that gets the girl every time. Eventually, *she'll* crave another man. So these two parts of me (wife and addictgirl) fight for control of one body.

Maybe the solution is to dispose of the body.

So after the crash-land with the blue convertible, I stop on a dime. Turn around. I no longer have sex. None. I eliminate men. I ration what I eat as if the world's food supply is toxic. I am in total control, obsessed with the job of my body's annihilation. Until I barely think about this troublesome body.

I don't miss it.

Only this state of celibacy can cleanse me. Only the state of starvation (no fat, no nutrients, no protein, no carbohydrates) can dissolve my lungs, rinse my mind, drain my heart, formaldehyde the remains. On this carefully tended, emaciated body, I wear plain oxford shirts buttoned tight to the collar. I slumber in the pure essence of arctic isolation—thin air, no food, no sounds, no sex, no color—an anorexic, monochromatic world with nothing of the real world to tempt me. I am a one-woman famine.

While in Galveston, my husband and I live on the Strand. We have an apartment on the top floor of a restored Victorian ironfront building, near the wharf and bars, where once I prowled. Now snatches of music from down the street waft up to me. Bar doors slam. Faint drunken shouts. Sounds that once enticed, exhaust me. Nor do I have the energy to dine out with my husband and his clients. I don't see friends. I call in sick to work. Without my neon hum of addiction, I *am* sick: hungover.

I'm neither wife nor addictgirl. Only wasted.

Days, I lie on the couch. Summer sun seems to warp the panes of the high-arched windows. Hard light straight from the skylight disfigures rather than clarifies. Even in the silence of empty days and dry nights, I don't understand who I am, why I am here, or what is wrong.

On one particular day I hear the ground-floor entry door open and shut. Footsteps come up wooden stairs. The sound echoes against the brick walls. I think I feel a thin vibration in the glass of the windows and skylight, in the glass of the interior atrium that plunges from the roof of the building down to the courtyard.

The footsteps pass the second-story landing and continue up.

The footsteps seem familiar and unfamiliar, both at the same time. Yet I'm expecting no one. I lift my head and watch the atrium windows. A man's head. A young man in a uniform walks with authority up the stairs and across the landing to my apartment.

The uniform of an exterminator? There are no bugs. A man reading a meter? The meters are outside. A plumber? No drains are clogged. I have called no one, invited no one over.

He raps on the door.

The door, I know, is unlocked. I never bother to lock it.

I glance at my body, at what I am wearing. A blue and white robe tied at the waist. I have not been out today. I have not bothered dressing.

The knob turns.

I sit up.

The door opens.

I stand up.

He walks in.

Khaki uniform, neatly pressed and starched, sharp creases down the pants legs. The name of a company is stitched in red thread across the shirt pocket.

I don't speak.

He sees me. His eyebrows rise. His lips part. His expression registers surprise.

Mine does not. I am not surprised to see a strange man standing in my apartment, me barefoot in a robe.

My heart does not race. My pulse does not quicken. My knees do not weaken.

His dark skin and hair seem like a comforting shadow softening the light of the apartment, the glare and glassy heat of withdrawal.

He mumbles something. "The landlord had called . . ." I don't quite hear what he says.

I have not moved forward, toward him, or backward, away from him.

He is the one to flee. His footsteps quickly thud down three flights of stairs.

The door off the courtyard slams shut and footsteps pound, racing, fading down the sidewalk.

At first I think he is the one who is legitimate and that I am the one to confuse him, that he thinks *I* am burglar or rapist. I am the one in the state of dishabille, after all.

Long moments pass before I realize *he* is the burglar, assuming everyone would be out during the day.

Weeks later, in thick summer heat, I drive my unair-conditioned Volkswagen past wilted oleanders toward the Gulf in search of a breeze. A black car in front of me runs a stop sign, and another car smashes into it. I *see* the shatter of glass, the puncture of metal, see cars whip sideways, an oil stain darkening the pavement. I even think I see collapsed bodies.

But the accident seems distant. For I *hear* no crash. I feel no crash. I hear no screams or shouts for help. The accident seems to have occurred on some other plane of existence.

And because I hear nothing and feel nothing, I continue on in search of a breeze. Calmly, truly calmly, I put my Volkswagen in first gear and negotiate around the pile of cars. The accident is not something I am capable of recognizing or feeling.

I park on the seawall and stand on the jetty waiting for the breeze to find me. In the sheen of light and water, the air is bleached and blinding. The Gulf hardens to aluminum glitter, the sun a feverish hole in the sky.

I am here in Galveston, but also seem to see a past decade, a different island, another sea—the Caribbean Sea in the West Indies—where I lived for a while as a child. Back then, I used to stand on the veranda of our house on Blackbeard's Hill and watch trade winds drift toward me, gathering velocity from across the sea. When their massive presence reached me, I felt as if I were carried far away by wind currents, until I could no longer see my house or my mahogany bed, no longer sense my drowsy body or feel the ruffle of the mosquito net that veiled my father and me.

There must be a connection between the trade winds in the West Indies—and this breeze I wait for now.

But here on the Galveston jetty, I am too numb to understand how these decades link together. I am unable to glue the past and present together into a mosaic of understanding, not wanting to acknowledge that this wreck of a girl in the present is a mutation from the wreck of her childhood. So there is no reason to be here today: no breeze, no comfort, nothing. I return home.

I never tell my husband about the burglar. Nor did I stop to make sure an ambulance arrived at the car crash. It's not as if I wanted the intruder to rape or steal. It's not as if I didn't want to help those strangers at the accident. I simply do not know how to react to dangerous emergencies, I now realize. Neither event seems extraordinary or even out of the ordinary. I do not know how to register fear, I think, calmly. Still very calm.

Now I briefly remember that I did not know to say the word *help* on that snowy sidewalk outside the Ritz-Carlton, either. Nor did I know how to say the word *help* in my childhood bedrooms. And now, as if the hem of a gauzy curtain lifts to reveal one thin ray of a much larger truth, I see that after all these years I still do not know how to form that word *help*. More: I do not know how to determine when I am in trouble.

So day after day in Galveston, I begin to miss the energy of that other woman who cruised streets and bars. I miss her power. Even if her energy causes my own emotional crash-landings in blue convertibles, it feels more alive and solid than this body. I feel as if all my senses have drained from the top of my head down to the soles of my feet.

I spend long days wishing for a transmigration.

Even as I don't want to be *her*, that other woman.

It's just that I want to be someone. Someone who walks, smells, tastes, thinks. I want to speak. Except, even with all the words I have spoken, all the words I have spoken about love, I don't know or understand so much as one true definition of love's vocabulary. I have never let anyone see an exposed, emotionally valid me.

And then, I realize, I don't know how to react to dangerous emergencies because *I* am the dangerous emergency.

How can I distinguish a car crash if *I* am the car crash?

This is when, in Galveston, I first consider a therapist. He (it must be a "he") will help me find the real me. I must also see a male therapist because this, I convince myself, will be a safe seduction, with a safe man.

To me this is a rational plan.

So therapy, like my anorexic life, is a sham. I blaze my way through four therapists in a year until I settle on one my addictwoman wants (but fails) to seduce, one of ten therapists I will eventually want (but will fail) to seduce.

However, this particular psychiatrist does not encourage me to talk about feelings or childhoods, what I don't understand anyway. Nor, when I arrive at his office in flimsy, filmy clothes, does he order me home to change. He does not teach me to come to therapy or approach life as an appropriately dressed sober adult woman.

Rather, month after month, I wear my dressed-to-seduce addict mask to his office until, once again, I have absorbed its properties, until, again, I am transformed to addict and no longer remember how to impersonate an ordinary woman.

To this psychiatrist I talk about seduction. He listens. To me, obsessing about sex with this therapist is the quiddity of addiction, is as good as a physical seduction. Because from the way he watches me, I believe I seduce with words if not with actions. My words, I believe, can be as good as actions. Here in his darkened office, with shades drawn and lights low, I tell him about the motel rooms, the bodies. I never get better because neither he nor any of the other therapists *knows* I am an addict. All they see is a woman who's depressed. They feed me antidepressants and don't understand a pill won't fix me. The language of depression won't cure this disease. Only language to dispel the addict will cure me. Ted, my eleventh therapist, is the first and only one who recognizes me. Ted is the only one who recognizes the addictwoman as well as who I want to be without her. Ted is the only therapist who tries to teach me sobriety. He is the only therapist who makes me confront my addict's most terrifying image: what I look like sober.

Every time. Every man. Every encounter . . . I end up alone in the real Rainbow Motel, or in the Rainbow Motel of my mind. Only sobriety will stop this. Sobriety. One word. Four syllables.

I have never before done this, but now in room #213 I must. I pick up the phone to call Ted at his home. I have never seen his home, can't even imagine it. Now, when I hear him say hello, this is the time I must tell him what he needs to know. Now I must tell him the only word he really needs to hear me speak to explain why I left the unit. I whisper the word, the one I tried to speak into his answering machine. I will break the promise I made Gabriel.

"Gabriel."

In a rush, because he might hang up, I tell him about Gabriel coming to my room, about our conversation in the museum. Yet I also try to convince Ted that nothing about this was sexual. I tell him I was with Rick today, that I left the unit because I thought Jill met Gabriel in the lounge. "Nothing much really happened." I don't want to remember Gabriel's hand on my shoulder or his palm on my collarbone when I sat on the bench in the museum.

"This doesn't sound like 'nothing.'" Ted's voice is quiet.

I balance the phone between my jaw and shoulder. I wrap the bedspread around me again and press the knuckles of one hand against the knuckles of the other until I feel bone. "But I thought I loved him."

"Love doesn't result in sitting alone in motel rooms," he says. "Addiction results in sitting alone in motel rooms."

I can't hear this. I don't want to know this. I slide from the bed onto the floor. Now, faced with being alone, I whisper, "I don't know if I can stop."

Faintly, through the receiver, I hear Ted's television. And I wish I was with Ted, just an ordinary person watching television.

"You're killing yourself." His voice is so low I barely hear him. "You have to stop."

"I always thought that intensity meant I was alive."

"*This*, what you're feeling *now*, is being alive."

"Oh."

DAY THIRTEEN

GABRIEL IS FIRED.

These are the words Ted says to begin group. Ted seems more upset than I've ever seen him, more, even, than when I've told him I've acted out. His skin is pale, his mouth tense. He explains that the director of personnel, who hired Gabriel, had a long talk with Gabriel and even refused to recommend him for another job. Ted apologizes for not providing a safer place for us to recover. He also feels sad that Jill and I couldn't tell him about meeting Gabriel, and hopes that if any of us need help in the future we'll take responsibility for ourselves and let him know.

I am sitting on the floor, leaning against the side of the

couch. "But how can you help me, why should I even stay, if I wasn't safe here to begin with?" I say.

"I am really so very sorry," Ted says. "But I think, if you let us"—he indicates the unit, the other women, him—"we can still help you. I hope you'll let us try."

"How, if *you* couldn't even see who he was?" I say. "You and the rest of the staff are therapists."

"Guess I'm a *human* therapist," he says. "We make mistakes, too. This is a big one, I know. But I'm afraid you're going to have to accept an imperfect therapist. An imperfect world."

Not to excuse himself, but Ted also explains that he has nothing to do with hiring at the hospital. He never saw Gabriel's application or reviewed his history—what other jobs he had—whether there'd been previous problems that were overlooked. He said, in fact, he had little contact with Gabriel, since the nurses arranged Gabriel's schedule. "Still," he adds, "I should have been more observant. I was fooled by Gabriel, too."

"Sounds like Gabriel should've been a patient, not a staffer," Sheila says.

"I'm afraid you're right," Ted says. "And now I need a commitment from all of you never to have contact with Gabriel again. That means not in person or in writing, no letters, no telephone calls. No leaving messages on answering machines."

There is a murmur of yeses—from everyone but me.

"Talking to him on the phone, even if you're not talking

about sex, is 'mind fucking,'" Ted says. "Sex addiction isn't about sex. It's about power and control. It's about numbing feelings. Just like alcoholism isn't about alcohol and eating disorders aren't about food."

Ted turns to me. "I need a commitment from you, too. Maybe you want to let us know how you feel with him gone?"

Devastated. Bereft. Inconsolable. Desolated. I also feel hungover. My throat feels raw, my heart chafed and humid. "Maybe you should have at least given Gabriel another chance," I say. "Like you give us, when we act out. Guess I'm not sure I should have told you in the first place."

Yet I'm stunned by my contradictions, my hypocrisy. For as angry as I am at the hospital for hiring Gabriel, I'm equally angry they fired him. And worried he's angry at me because of it.

"You can't have it both ways," Ted says. "There's no way for both you *and* your addict to be okay with this. You did the right thing to tell me. Don't you want to get better?"

How can I possibly want Gabriel, or even Rick, more than I want to get better? "I don't know," I say.

"I'd feel sad if you're letting your addict make decisions for you." His voice is slow and earnest. "But I also know there's no way I can help you if you don't want to be helped."

Help. I feel a flush spread up my neck to my cheeks. The one word I need; the one sentiment I've never been able to ask for.

Ted writes on his legal pad. I suspect the worst. A black mark next to my name. A demerit. "Look," Ted says, "just because we call an addiction a disease doesn't mean you can give in to it. It means you have to be more powerful than it—with the help of others. With the help of the group." He looks at me. "My hope is that you might learn from this— learn how to keep yourself safe—even when you're not in a safe situation."

"Yesterday, I left in the first place because it wasn't safe. *Here*."

"You left here because you thought *I* was with Gabriel," Jill says.

"Weren't you?" I say.

"What if I was?" she says. "You don't own him." On the coffee table is a clear plastic box, a knickknack, containing different-colored sands. She picks it up and tips it back and forth, watching sand rearrange itself. "Christ, he's just another man."

I stand and take a step toward the door. "This place *still* isn't safe," I say to Ted, but nodding toward Jill.

"I suspect if you leave here you'll go see Gabriel," Ted says. "And that puts me in a real bind because I can't let you do that."

"They only lock up people who're going to kill themselves," I say. "Or someone else."

"And that's what you'll be doing if you leave here and see Gabriel."

"Sex isn't suicidal. Or homicidal."

"It is for you," he says.

The message on Gabriel's answering machine says: "Haste is the enemy of knowledge. Please leave a message, a way to get back in touch, and as soon as possible, I will."

Again, I am alone in the unoccupied room across from the lounge. I depress the plunger on the telephone but hold on to the receiver. I wonder where he is, whom he is with, at four o'clock in the morning.

I must apologize to Gabriel for telling Ted. I must know whether he's angry at me. I must ask him to forgive me.

I release the plunger. I listen to the dial tone, a comforting connection, as if this path of sound leads only to his house, to his phone, to him. I must talk to him. I must talk to him *now*. "Haste is the enemy of knowledge." Strange message for an addict. A message on my answering machine might say: "I want what I want when I want it."

I redial his number. The moment I say my name I hear his voice, his *real* voice, having screened the call. For a moment I am uncertain what to say to the real him. What is the perfect phrase to ensure he will forgive me, love me, desire me, always interrupt his answering machine at the sound of my voice?

"I'm really sorry," I say. "I only left the unit, and everything happened, because I thought you were with Jill."

"I got delayed getting to the unit," he says. "And then I found her, not you."

"Oh. I see. I'm so sorry I told Ted."

"If you'd waited another ten minutes, we would have

met." His voice is blunt with anger. "Instead, you got me fired."

"You want me to talk to that director of personnel?" I say. "I'll tell them this was all a mistake. Anything."

"Forget it. The real problem is this bullshit, puritanical society. Ted and them just want you to conform to the same stupid rules. You must not be ready for me, all we wanted to share."

"But I *am* ready," I say. "I just kind of freaked out about you and Jill."

"Remember that note I gave you?"

The only infallible, immutable, unlimited power that heals, without question, is love. "Yes."

"Jill needs a lot of healing, too."

"You mean loving," I say.

"We all need loving."

But to you, to Jill, loving is fucking, I think. "And you . . . heal her."

"I want to heal all of us," he says. "I thought you wanted that, too."

You want to fuck all of us, I think. "I *do*."

"I'd imagined such beautiful things with you." His voice is slow, dark, serious. "This isn't about sex, you know."

But it isn't not about sex. "I wish—if we were together . . ."

"We are," he says. "We *can* be. Tell me what we're doing."

I slide down on the bed and lean my head against the pillow. I know what he needs to hear in order for all to be forgiven. My tone is low, seductive. "I see us . . . I see me, there

with you in your bedroom," I say. "I bet you have black silk
sheets. . . ." I feel the diminishment of my real self, while this
addict self, fake, conjures this fantasy in order to please him.
This, what I want to do.

DAY
FOURTEEN

I DON'T FEEL LIKE writing in my Workbook. No, I feel like writing—but about Gabriel. I want to record every word of our conversation last night. I want to save it, reread it, feel as if I'm injecting it into a tied-off vein.

Linda pushes open the door, holding her own Workbook, and flops onto my bed. "Have you done that section about family histories yet?" she asks. I shake my head. "Well, I just figured out this stuff about 'sisters,'" she says, "why it's so hard to be one." Linda looks at me: direct and steady. "Like, *my* sister is a lot prettier than me, and when she was a teenager, and I was still a kid, when she dressed up and looked sexy, our father'd watch her and follow her around the house—and I used to hate *her*. When I should have been angry at *him*. *That's* how I got all this stuff confused. And I still haven't forgiven *her*."

"*Sisters*," Jill says. She's on the floor, doing leg lifts. "That's nothing. My kid sister ran away from home at fourteen."

"That's awful," Linda says. "What happened?"

"Who knows?" Jill shrugs. "It was ages ago. And I'm not the one with the problem, anyway. I always got more attention than Jesse. I'm prettier than she is, too."

"But you're here. Your sister's gone. No way you're going to convince me everything was fine," I say.

"Besides, what did your father do to show his 'love'?" Linda asks. "It must've been bad. He messed up both of you."

Jill does one more leg lift, then stretches her muscles. "Nothing."

"Then why won't you talk about it?" Linda asks. "Don't you miss her? Or are you jealous of her—like with me and my sister?"

"Neither," Jill says.

Both, I suspect.

"But don't you want to find Jesse?" I say.

I think of my own sister. I know where she is; I know where she lives, yet we still don't know each other. She jogs two hours a day . . . running just the way she ran off with her friends when we were young. I always missed her. I was also jealous of her freedom: the ease with which she seemed to escape our house. Yet now I wonder if she floated away *too* easily; for in our family there wasn't enough love to bind her to it.

Except, ironically, none of us ever really escaped our parents—or their lessons. We also didn't escape the lessons they failed to teach us: because our parents didn't know how to be parents, they didn't know how to teach us to be sisters, mothers, wives.

"My sister . . ." Jill takes a deep breath and sighs. She pulls the sweatband from her hair and turns it absently.

If only Jill could *always* be this thoughtful, this still. *This* is who I want Jill to be. This is who *I* want to be.

Again, I want to tell her the truth: that I did try to call her when she left the unit.

But I know how little it would take for this moment to be interrupted, for her mask to fall back in place.

So, still, I don't tell her the truth.

DAY FIFTEEN

"THERE'S A SKYLIGHT above my bed," Gabriel says to me on the phone.

Again I have called him, after midnight, using the phone in the empty room across from the lounge. I had to.

"This is where I first see you," he says. "As if there's no glass, you float down to me."

"What would happen when I reach you?" I ask.

"I would tie you with white ribbons."

"But then I wouldn't be free."

"*Imagine* that submission can be the highest form of freedom," he says.

"How can you be so different from Ted?"

"How can you not imagine? We probably act less, the freer the imagination."

"With Ted everything is literal. I always know what he means."

"Even the 'literal' world is subjective."

I don't have to be part of Gabriel's dayworld to be part of his nightworld. Part of his dreamworld. Does the image of me in his mind resemble my dayworld self? Maybe I am an afterimage.

"Sex doesn't have to be what Ted tells you," he says. "Just *imagine* it different. Imagine sex is freedom. What makes you feel alive."

"It used to make me feel like I was dying."

"Sometimes our old selves *have* to die before we can grow new ones."

I can't tell Ted that I call Gabriel. If I do, they'll remove the phones. Not that Gabriel needs to hear my real voice. He could imagine its pitch and tone and be able to imagine all of me.

The same is true for me. I don't need the real Gabriel, either. In my own addictive creations, when I smell jasmine I taste Gabriel. When I see white bird feathers I feel Gabriel. I touch cool silver and turquoise and see Gabriel. It takes so little and yields so much.

"Christ, what's wrong?" Jill asks. When I return to my room, Jill has just walked out of the bathroom. She wears a cotton robe and no slippers. Her purple toenails seem too wide awake, almost alarmed, in the middle of the night, in the solitary light.

"Nothing," I say quickly, caught off guard by her sudden presence.

"You look awful," she says. "Must be something."

"Just insomnia."

She gets into bed. "What'd you do, call Gabriel?"

I cross the room and turn off the light. "Really, it's nothing."

"Christ, everyone's dumping on me around here for not acting like a 'sister,'" she says. "I had you all wrong. Guess I thought you were the kind of girl who wanted to get close and tell secrets."

"Okay, okay," I say. "I called Gabriel. You happy?"

I regret telling her.

I suspect that, albeit unconsciously, she shows just enough interest in me, in a friendship, in order to seduce me into liking her. And the moment when I feel closest, when I like her the most—at *that* moment—she will walk out the door for good.

DAY
SIXTEEN

THE NEXT NIGHT the message on Gabriel's answering machine says: "The person with the big dreams is more powerful than the one with all the facts."

Since he screens his calls, I humiliate myself and announce my presence, leave a message, not once, not twice. I call him at one o'clock in the morning. Two. Three. He is either out all night or not answering. If I confessed to Ted, he would tell me that Gabriel will answer his phone, answer my message, when he needs another fix. Ted would say, "Gabriel's 'big dreams' are to steal women's souls and bodies."

And *this* is the fact.

I ignore facts.

I continue to sit beside the phone—as if it might ring, as if he might call me.

DAY
SEVENTEEN

TED AND I SIT in the lounge for an individual session. I am not speaking, and he is patiently waiting. On his coffee mug the word *coffee* is printed in numerous languages such as Spanish, French, Italian, English. How simple, I think. How ordinary. The word *coffee* is simple and ordinary. And the manufacturer is so thoughtful to print the word in so many languages, cover all international bases. You know when you pick up the mug what you are drinking. In any language. No surprise.

In a gentle way Ted's eyes try to read me—no, interpret me, or translate *me* into his own basic language where the word *coffee* always means "coffee." Literally.

"I don't think I quite understand reality," I say. I try to explain how my imagination, my fantasies, seem as real, say, as Ted's coffee mug. "Like if you're doing drugs or something and have a hallucinogenic experience, are those perceptions real?"

"I think those perceptions are trance-induced delusions," he says. "But addicts become so involved with them that the delusions *become* their reality. But in your sense, the way you mean it, no, not real."

"But isn't it just a different kind of reality?"

"When you were young, and your father hurt you, you changed reality by *believing* what he did was love. Then, that was the only way you had to survive the pain. So it was good, in that at least it kept you alive." Yet that false belief was the beginning of the addict persona, he explains, which now has become so pervasive that it's *bad*. "Now the addict creates a powerful and false distraction that inhibits your ability to live real life—or to resolve legitimate pain—such as your past."

Yes, addictions keep all of us alive until, ironically, they kill us. Over the years, addicts become more hard-core. In my delusional belief that dangerous men love me, I re-create the past. It is the only thing to which I have been faithful.

"*This* is the only real world I know." Ted nods at the lounge, at the unit, meaning the tangible world we see before us.

In Ted's real world, the word *coffee*, therefore, remains one word, one substance. A minimalist approach to language. In Ted's world less is more. Less is less is even better.

In addiction more is more. Hyperbole, exaggeration, connotation are even better, where the word *coffee*, for example, could connote man, woman, steaming cups of coffee spiked with rum, a thick rug beside a fireplace, discarded ski sweaters, a winter dusk with air dark as plums. In other words, even the word *coffee* could connote the word *sex*.

Ted says, "Now, how about if we move on to what we're *not* talking about?" I look away, guilty. "Have you tried calling Gabriel?"

I pick up the plastic box filled with sand and tip it over.

"No," I say.

"You keeping him in your mind, like a stash?" He waits. "I mean, I know how hard it is to change habits."

Change.

Right before Ted said the word *change* he exhaled, so the word seemed to burst from his mouth.

Of course I know that I entered treatment in order to try to change. Yet in the way Ted uttered the word *change*, it's as if I hear the word for the very first time.

I can change. Can I change? Flip a lever, flip a switch. That simple, that easy. And I will no longer even think about calling Gabriel.

Change: Behavior. Clothes. Language. Thoughts. Me.

But suppose I can't change?

And suddenly the word and its meaning—*that I am capable of change*—is so terrifying that my addict absolutely does not want me to know this word, does not want me to change. Yes, as Ted said: it *does* want to keep me trapped in bad behaviors.

Ted persists. "You might be surprised by how powerful you feel if you focus on *your* feelings," he says. "Not theirs. Put that energy into understanding yourself. You already know those men."

I tuck my legs onto the chair and lean my head back, exhausted just thinking about the words *power* and *change*. "Suppose I'm nothing without them," I say.

The clarity of his blue eyes urges me to understand his truth rather than my own unreason. "You aren't."

He hands me a pass to have dinner with Andrew—a week from now. Since I live too far away to drive home, Ted suggests that Andrew and I meet at a restaurant in Atlanta. Instructions accompany the pass: I am to drive directly to the restaurant and back. No detours. I am to be back at the unit no later than ten P.M.

I watch Ted with steady eyes. I am capable of following the instructions. To follow the instructions implies I can change.

My addict glances at Ted and smiles. I am not capable of following the instructions. On my way back to the unit I will visit Gabriel. I am not capable of changing.

"Ted, wait." I drop the pass on the coffee table. "I don't want it. I'm not ready."

"The other day you could hardly wait to get out of here."

"I *know*. But Gabriel—"

"Afraid you'll visit him?"

"Yes. No. I don't know."

He smiles. "That's honest, anyway."

"I just keep thinking—suppose, just suppose he's different.

Suppose he's a dangerous man who *is* spiritually capable of loving me. Then both my addict *and* I could be happy."

"Whether he's spiritual or not—and I suspect he's not—you're still 'using' his spirituality as an excuse to act out with him. He knew you would. And maybe he tries to create that illusion. It's like when you wear your addict clothes—or flirt at parties—that persona." He leans forward as if I might better understand what he is saying. "Besides, pretending these men love you isn't going to make it happen. You don't love them, either."

I don't love them, either. "I don't?"

"Do you?"

"Gosh, I mean, no, of course not. I mean, I can fall in love with a man because of the way he looks in *sunglasses*."

"Speaking of reality—"

"I guess 'sunglasses' aren't exactly valid barometers of love."

"If you 'create' these men in your head, you can 'uncreate' them just as easily. They're just *men*. They may be dangerous, but *you're* the one who gives them that power and that quality. *You* make them into something they're not. They're not Greek gods or superheroes or mythical creatures. They're just ordinary. Regular guys. Just men."

"Just men."

"Besides," Ted adds, "why *didn't* you have sex with Gabriel? What stopped you?"

"Well, he didn't show up that night."

"What else?"

"I didn't—don't—even want to have sex with him," I say,

without thinking, almost before I realize what I'm saying. "It
is about control. You're right. But when I think that he, or
any man, desires me, I have some. And I feel so powerful."

Ted settles back in his chair. "Most sex addicts don't like
sex—any more than alcoholics like alcohol." The tone of his
voice says: Hear me, believe me, listen. "You tell yourselves
you like it, whatever the addiction. But why would anyone
like something that's killing them?"

Ted picks up the pass and hands it to me again. I put it in
my pocket. I stand to go, but hesitate. Ted, about to write
something on his legal pad, glances up.

"I called Gabriel," I say.

"I know," he says.

"More than once."

"I know."

"How?"

"You're an addict," he says. "But I'm pleased you trust me
enough to tell me."

Still I pause. "It's just . . . it's so hard to say no to a man. If
he wants me."

"But hear what they're really asking you. What they're
really offering."

Nothing, I think. Less.

"You know," Ted adds, "one of these days you are going to
have to start dealing with Andrew. Get honest with him. Tell
him about these men. Your other life."

But he'll leave me. Hate me. I'd feel so ashamed.

"You might want to start trying when you meet him for
dinner."

DAY
EIGHTEEN

"THEY'RE SO PEACEFUL," Linda says. On our field trip to ZooAtlanta, Jill, Linda, and I are watching flamingos perched on reedy legs. Loose feathers skim the pond in a pink wash. "Maybe I should have a flamingo as my Higher Power," she adds.

"What animal would you choose?" I ask Jill.

"Snakes," she says. One word, one harsh syllable, no surprise.

A flamingo winds its neck around the side of its body to scratch its plumage with its beak. "Wow—think of the oral sex," Jill says. "With those necks." She turns and walks away.

"Sometimes I just can't stand her," Linda says. "You know?"

"Yeah. But for me, I guess it's just that I understand her." Understand a woman who uses sex, or jokes, or anger, or secrets, or lies in order to keep everybody—who might want to get close to the real her—away. Understand a woman whose father might have hurt her and her sister. Understand a woman who's afraid to get close to another woman.

Linda and I follow our group (we're all here except Pole Lady) down a path edged with azaleas. I wonder if families we pass, children, watch us. On the surface we must seem discordant—fat/skinny, elaborately dressed/elaborately plain. I shuffle my feet, ragged shoelaces trailing. Linda floats in tie-dye, bells on her skirt tinkling. Sheila trudges with the weight of her shame. Jill pulses in primary-colored energy. Two teenage boys watch her. She pretends not to notice. I know she notices. Yes, I understand how even a fleeting high is better than no high. After all, why else would she wear tight red-red denims that say: "I want to fuck"?

Except, regardless of appearance, we are all really alike. For we carry our lunches in brown paper sacks, wayward children, yes, lunches fixed by adults who know how to nourish us, for none of us learned to nourish ourselves.

We lean elbows on the warm iron rail of a cement enclosure where a polar bear hunkers in shallow water. He must be endlessly dismayed to find himself in humid Georgia. The bear, too, must learn the lessons of the trance. Then, transported to the Arctic, to imaginary ice, he would dissociate from boredom and heat. I stare at him as if I can will him northward via genetic memory.

I sit on a nearby bench. A family of four strolls past. The young son wears a red plastic cowboy hat and ripped jeans. His sister wears yellow sneakers with electric-green laces and is licking an ice-cream cone. The boy is shrieking and racing around to attract the polar bear's attention. He holds out his fist like a gun and "shoots" it. The bear, perhaps lost to Arctic memory, climbs onto a rocky ledge, stoic, and doesn't flinch.

I, too, drift to other times and places. I see this image of the boy, ordinary, anyboy. But the image subverts to Jeffrey Dahmer. And now I want to know if *he* ever represented everyboy. Surely, once, he did. I want to stop time. At that moment. I want to hold Jeffrey Dahmer's hand . . . *but that little-boy hand* . . . and lead him in another direction. Bring him, say, to the zoo. Then he could grow to be an ordinary man and not have to invent himself into a creation he wasn't meant to be.

Linda sits beside me, followed by Jill.

"You ever think about Jeffrey Dahmer?" I say. "You know, that cannibal."

"How can you *eat* people!" Linda says.

Jill pushes her sunglasses up on her head. "I like cock on the grill."

"With Heinz barbecue sauce," I say.

"Too many calories," Linda says.

"We could write a cookbook," I say.

"*Joy of Cooking*, by Jeffrey Dahmer," Jill says.

The little girl with electric-green shoelaces begins to

scream. Apparently her brother grabbed her ice-cream cone. Sobbing, she tries to kick him.

"Man, I can think of a couple of kids I'd like to burn to a crisp right now," Jill says, nodding toward the children.

"How you think he figured his temperatures?" Linda says.

"In a Kenmore," Jill says.

I begin to laugh. So do Jill and Linda. For me it is the ordinariness of the word *Kenmore* that has brought me to laughter. While the laugh starts slow, it seems to grow as if coming from far away. We laugh harder. Almost shrill. Just this side of hysteria. Jill, in her own hysteria, can't stop talking as she's laughing, rattling off rhymes about Jeffrey Dahmer, riffing on his deeds. The sunglasses, pushed up on her head, reflect light, and she seems to be all bright eyes, all energy and sun and dazzle.

"Sorry I butchered your son. We really had a great deal of fun. I devoured his entrails, his spine, and his toenails—"

"Wait," Linda says. "I got one. Your son was the pick of the deli. . . ."

"He tastes better than ham," Jill says.

"Or containers of Spam," I say.

"And his blood brewed into the finest of jellies."

As our laughter fades, Linda sighs. I look back at that polar bear, who makes a few halfhearted stabs at swimming in warm water.

"I bet that bear's really pissed he's not in the Arctic," I say.

"He can join group and work through his anger," Jill says. She slides her sunglasses back until they rest on the bridge of her nose.

The rest of our group is heading toward a grassy area to eat lunch, and Nancy, our chaperone-nurse, motions to us to follow. We sit under oak trees and open packages of chicken salad sandwiches, potato chips, and bottles of fruit juice. I stretch out my legs and feel breeze, sun, shadow. Overhead, small, ordinary birds, not exotic birds, flap their wings in everyday sunlight.

Why do I believe Jeffrey Dahmer never felt this?

I put down my sandwich and lean forward. And I make myself, absolutely make myself, stare at the grass, stare at an oak leaf, at a wrapper of Wrigley's spearmint gum. Just see this, I say to myself. See the ordinary—the word Ted used yesterday to describe men.

Linda is reading the ingredients on the back of the package of potato chips, checking the fat and calorie content, I know.

Once again Jill has pushed up her sunglasses and is staring past our group to a family sitting nearby on a blanket . . . no . . . I follow the path of her gaze. She watches the father, the husband, who quickly glances at her—then away.

"Jill, Linda," I say—and try to explain what I've been thinking. "I mean, Ted is right. It's about seeing ordinary things." I motion toward the man with his family. "I mean, why can't we just see an ordinary man without creating some fantasy?"

"It's not a 'we,'" Jill says. "It's a 'you.' If you think a fucking blade of grass is more interesting than . . ." she shrugs. "Whatever."

"But you *know* we are the only people at the zoo today talking about Jeffrey Dahmer."

Jill squashes her empty bag of chips and plastic wrappers and jams them into the sack. "So, like, what are they talking about? Their 'Martha Stewart' houses? Christ, Martha Stewart is as obsessive-compulsive as Jeffrey Dahmer. Just think how she'd arrange severed heads on fancy platters."

"Can't you guys stop it?" Linda says. "Can't we pretend we're normal for one afternoon?"

We stand behind a glass partition overlooking the gorillas. A mother gorilla sits on the ground under a tree holding her baby. Another gorilla, about the age of a toddler, sits at his mother's feet, yanking grass. Higher up the hill a male gorilla swings from a rope attached to the limb of a tree.

"Haven't male gorillas gotten the message?" Linda says. "That they're supposed to share child-rearing responsibilities?"

The toddler gorilla tries to climb onto his mother's lap. She pushes him off. He makes a *squawk-clack* sound and tries again. Again she pushes him off, cradling her infant in the crook of her arm. The toddler sits by her feet watching her. Then he inches closer. Again he nudges his mother's lap. Again she pushes him off. *Squawk-clack. Squawk-clack.* The toddler waves his arms, then grabs a low branch of the tree. He begins to swing on it before climbing to the end, where he hangs for a moment. Then, slowly, he lowers himself toward his mother. At first his mother tolerates him as he slides onto her shoulders, but then she shakes her arm until he falls off.

"Why can't she just hold both of them?" I say. "I mean, what is her problem?"

"Her kid is going to have major abandonment issues," Jill says. "He'll probably start bingeing on bananas."

"He'll need a Twelve-Step group."

"Hi, I'm Kong," Jill says. "I'm a bananaholic."

"Hi, Kong," Linda and I say in unison.

Now the toddler is hopping around his mother, clapping his hands, his cry shrill and severe. Over and over he leaps onto her thigh, and over and over she swats him off.

"Let's get out of here," Linda says. "I can't stand it."

We follow a path to a field of three elephants. Next to us a little girl with black pigtails sits on her father's shoulders, her forearms on top of his head. I think she looks familiar. . . . I glance at Jill. She, too, watches the girl. Yes, that photograph of her sister, Jesse. This girl, about the same age as Jesse in that picture, has similar features. Jill is still now, for the first time today, not even noticing the girl's father. I want to say something, but I know with one word her sunglasses will be slammed down over her eyes.

Because I watch Jill, I don't fully see what happens with the elephant. Either the elephant closest to us has stumbled, or he hurt his trunk on the fence. He bobs his head up and down while his ears flap.

But the instant he cries out, the other two elephants, in a lumbering gallop, rush to the wounded elephant's side. They hover close together as if discussing what happened. The two sweep their trunks across the hurt elephant's sides, caressing him. *Does it hurt here? Does it hurt here?* Their trunks trail the length of the hurt elephant's body. Their bodies brush one another. Their ears flap.

Soon the elephants calm down. The hurt elephant seems fine—a minor injury. I glance at Jill. She is quieter than I've ever seen her, no sexual tilt to her head. Quiet—perhaps because of the girl in pigtails, perhaps because of the polar bear, the gorillas, the elephants. She clasps the rail of the enclosure, almost as if she wants to climb over. To help the elephants? To free them?

"I wonder where it's safer," I say, "locked up or out here in the world?"

"I was just thinking about a whole herd of elephants just galumphing along through some old field in Africa," Jill says.

"I'd love to go to Africa," Linda says. "And see them."

Nancy calls to us that it's time to leave. I start to follow, then notice Jill still watching the elephants. "Ready?" I say, reaching to touch her shoulder.

She turns to me, slowly. But in her slow, slow movement there is time to create, re-create, her image. She steps back. Just enough so my hand can't reach her.

Back on the unit, I notice the absence immediately. The absence of sound—before I notice her thin form is missing. No wheels creaking up and down the hall, usually as dependable as a bus schedule. Nothing. "Where *is* she?" I turn to Linda.

"Pole Lady?" she says. "Didn't you hear?" I shake my head.

"After she refused to go to the zoo, she ripped out the tubes. They had to put her on the medical unit."

I hurry down the hall to her room. I push open the door. She was the one patient not required to have a roommate, and the room is deserted. The pole is gone. And even though it was the staff who must have changed the sheets, still, the room is so vacant, the bed so neat, it's as if she was unwilling to commit so much as a wrinkle to the bedspread, wanting no evidence of her existence.

I never asked her her name.

I back out of the room and close the door. I return to my room, where Linda is sitting on the chair, Jill on her bed.

"She didn't *die*, did she?" I say.

Linda shakes her head. "Guess that's why they moved her. So she *wouldn't*."

I lie down on my bed and stare at the ceiling. "You know, when I first got here, checked in, I didn't expect them to search me, weigh me, all that stuff," I say. "I mean, what's the big deal if I packed a couple of razors. It was all sort of a joke—like one lighthearted romp through sex addiction."

"I know," Linda says. "Me, too."

"It's like I always use the word *danger*," I say, "except I conveniently ignore the fact that it's *living and dying* danger."

For a moment no one speaks. Then Jill says, "Guess that's why I always forget about condoms. I mean, I never thought those warnings applied to *me*."

I remember what Nancy said that day at breakfast, about eating one hundred percent. She reminded us that anorexics can die from heart attacks, sex addicts can die from AIDS—

SICKor mayhem and murder. And, yes, I suppose a small sober part of me must have considered, for example, that that obscene phone caller *could* have killed me. Or that man I drove away with in the Corvette. Those men in Galveston. But now I realize how forcefully my addict convinced me, instead, that risk was fun. Danger was bliss. Always, I needed what I needed—right then.

DAY
NINETEEN

FOR SPIRITUALITY GROUP, Ted instructs us to lie on the floor, close our eyes, and imagine. Relax our bodies, relax our minds, and imagine. Soothing sounds of a tropical rain forest play on the tape deck. Imagine we are seeds sprouting to seedlings. Imagine we are cocoons opening to butterflies. Birds warble. The rain forest drips.

Imagine a light. Follow this light to a place with no distractions, no temptations, no reminders, no addictions. Choose a guidebook or a trusted guide to follow, one that's spiritual. "A Higher Power doesn't have to be a god," Ted says. "It can be a tree, a star, an animal. Even the group."

Rather than use imagination as a destructive force that
imprisons us in addiction, turn the energy of imagination
into a force of safety, harmony, health, light.

What should I follow? Who? Ted's light? His blue eyes?
Elephants in a field in Africa? The guide must be stronger
than Rainbow Motels. Stronger than *liquid hot steel nights*,
that description I wrote of my addict in my Workbook.

When the tape ends, Ted hands out paper, crayons, glue,
ribbon, yarn, arts and crafts supplies. Now we are to draw
either images of our Higher Power or the safe places we
imagined. I ask for white posterboard and crayons. I listen to
murmuring women's voices, the tinkle of bells on Linda's
skirt. Scissors cutting. Pencils sketching. Women draw scenes
of rain forests, lakes, sunny beaches. Linda draws a flamingo.
Several women, including Sheila, paint angels. Sheila's angel
is as thin as one wing feather. Others draw cats and horses.
Jill sketches a can of Bud.

I sit on the floor and stare at my piece of posterboard. I
pick up a green and a blue crayon.

"Draw the ocean, a tree. Anything," Ted says to me. "Something outside yourself. There's a whole universe out there
that's stronger than the addiction."

Draw a universe.

But why color white posterboard? It is not what needs
emotional rearranging.

With the blue crayon I color the fingernails on my left
hand. With the green crayon, the nails on my right.

I hold out my arms.

Small, oblong planets? Green and blue wingtips?

But how easy to wipe the crayon off with the hem of my T-shirt.

I think of that woman in the SAA group who said she planted an oak to represent a Higher Power. I know an addict can uproot a sapling in one rageful storm.

"You having trouble?" Ted asks. He kneels beside me.

"Nothing's stronger than an addiction."

"Don't you think it loses some of its force after you write about it—what you've been doing in your Workbook for your First Step?"

"I guess," I say. "But I can't decide what to do with this." I nod toward the posterboard.

He picks up a black crayon and writes the word *MEN* on it. He hands me the crayon. I draw a large X through the word. I look up at him. Still, I'm not sure what he means.

"You say you like to write," he says.

"Words?"

He shrugs and smiles. "What do you think?"

So, then, it is the language to *describe* saplings, planets, universes. Language as a Higher Power. Language to describe an authentic me.

"Find your own language that has nothing to do with men's language," he says. "*Your* language—that's all *you*. See if it's stronger than the addiction."

Again I look at the posterboard.

It is a matter of labeling the men, labeling what I see and what I know.

Once I know the men's true names, once I chant their

names aloud, once I spell each of their names (including middle initial) with precision, once I translate their names using a dictionary named "Reality," then no longer will I wear their shadows. Then I can sleep with windows open to allow all their names to escape.

I sift through the box of supplies until I find a pen.

Starting with my father, I print on the posterboard the name of every dangerous man I have known. When I finish, I wipe the surface with a damp cloth. Ink dissolves. Names dissolve. Fading. Gone.

DAY
TWENTY

"YOU KNOW THAT Bazooka bubble gum?" Jill says.

"Not intimately," I say. After dinner we lie on our beds, bored, unable to think of a single thing to do.

"I would give up sex for, like, ten pieces of it right this second. Those little fat, pink squares are just so cute. All I can think about is stuffing as many as I can fit into my mouth all at once. You know how they're so gobby and chewy and mushy and how your mouth feels full of wads and wads of juicy sweet pink sugar."

"I'm about to go into a sugar coma just listening to you."

Jill gets up and empties the contents of her pocketbook on the bed, as if searching for gum. Amid keys, pens, lipsticks, she finds a stale Fig Newton. When she tries to bite it, it crumbles. "So what were you thinking about?" she asks.

"I don't know. That maybe the perfect relationship would be with a man who lives somewhere like Siberia."

"Yeah," Jill says. "You could feel like someone loved you. Without having to do anything about it." She picks up the pieces of Fig Newton and eats them.

"In fantasies you don't get abandoned," I say. "Or bored. Besides, what's the point of sex anyway? You even like it?"

Jill uncaps a lipstick and licks the top, maybe hoping it'll taste like gum. "I guess it's okay." She makes a face at the lipstick and returns her stuff to her purse. "I mean, there's always so much time. What else you gonna do?"

I think about what Ted told me the other day: that most sex addicts don't like sex.

Jill switches on the radio to the oldies station. She cranks it full volume. We listen to "Stop and Think It Over," "Be My Baby," "Did You Ever Have to Make Up Your Mind," "It Hurts to Be In Love," "Foolish Little Girl," "My Boyfriend's Back." Jill dances around the room, barely pausing between songs, singing off-key as loud as possible. "Do You Believe in Magic," "Bad Moon Rising," "(I Can't Get No) Satisfaction."

Linda, Sheila—one by one the women on the unit cram into our room and begin to bop around the floor. Linda pulls my hand, tugging me off the bed. By now we are all singing, badly. We don't stop moving, dancing, from one song into the next, laughing and screaming, mimicking motions of Motown groups we've seen on television, "Stop in the Name of Love." Linda's loose clothes swirl in time to rock 'n' roll music. Even though Sheila only sways, she waves her arms and snaps her fingers, keeping the beat.

When "Crying" comes on, we grab partners. Linda and I sway across the floor, exaggerating Roy Orbison's pain. At first, Jill dances alone. She twirls around the room from couple to couple. Then she grabs Sheila around the waist. She plays the role of male, leading her partner, coaxing Sheila to move faster and farther than I know Sheila has ever moved before.

Later that night, I hear women shuffle down the hall to watch television in the lounge. Voices. Laughter. I hear cars along the parkway. Sounds soothe. I remember lying in bed in my dorm in Boston, listening to girls laughing in the next room. Traffic on Storrow Drive. Back then, I didn't understand those ordinary sounds flowing smoothly through life.

DAY
TWENTY-ONE

TONIGHT AT THE SAA meeting Jim doesn't wear his seer-sucker suit. Instead, he wears a green and white polo shirt and denims. Even from where I sit across the room, I believe I see pale hairs on his forearms. I want to touch them. He watches me, too, and now I believe he no longer craves the woman in the red Camaro, the glimpsed woman he wanted to marry. In the egotism of my addiction, I believe he now dreams of me wearing a gown of ivory lace. Yes, Jim, it must be me. Because if I can't be with Gabriel . . . Jim, I now convince myself, since he attends SAA meetings, is safer than Gabriel.

"I'm Brad and I'm depressed. Except my therapist told

me that, in a way, depression doesn't even exist as a feeling, or that I, all of us, think it's depression, call it depression, but that it's really an addiction that's the problem."

Ted has told me the same thing: depression isn't a feeling that can be treated. Rather, depression is usually unresolved rage or anger or sadness turned inward and that it's impossible to resolve rage, anger, sadness as long as we are numbed out with food, with sex, with alcohol. Sober, we will finally feel sadness, fear, and be able to let them go. This can be the cure for depression.

"So I did some research on depression," Brad is saying. He holds up a piece of paper. "I read that fifty-three billion dollars is lost in the economy due to depression—mainly workers unable to work. And that clinical depression is the most disabling disease in the world." He puts the paper in his pocket. "So if all these people would get treated for addiction rather than depression, then they'd finally, *really*, be cured."

Jim no longer watches me, but I believe he senses me. I stretch out my legs in order to feel close to him. Jim, why don't we run up the stairs and out the door? You'll love me much more than the woman in the Camaro.

"My name is Steve and I'm a sex addict."

"Hi, Steve."

"When I woke up this morning I felt hungover. I was with my girlfriend last night, and we didn't have sex, but I don't know. We're working on this. We're trying not to have sex. We're trying to find ways to talk to each other instead and figure out the *I* word. Intimacy," he whispers.

Steve looks hungover. His scraggly hair is almost in his eyes. His plaid shirt is buttoned wrong and he seems exhausted.

"We used to have sex three, four times a day," he says. "But now, even just being with her, I still feel hungover. And it's really hard for me to go outside. I lost my job and I don't have any money and there's no reason to go out. But the thing of it is, I *want* to be with people. I want to learn how to connect with people, but I'm scared. Guess I think they won't like me if they really know me." He sighs and stares down. "But even *that's* not what's really bothering me." His voice softens. He says how, when he was a kid, he spied on his father masturbating in the basement, reading porno magazines. "It seemed so exciting and secretive. I wanted something like that in my own life. So I started stealing the magazines and masturbating, too. And even when I wasn't doing it, I'd *imagine* it—all day at school.

"So I never learned about normal sex. And even though society suggests we're supposed to have sex as much as possible, guess I'm finally learning that's *not* what *I* want anymore."

Donna says she's a drunk driver even though she doesn't drink alcohol. She cruises drive-throughs of McDonald's and eats burgers while driving, obsessed with food. In her addiction, she also scans streets and cars for sexy guys while driving. "Or I masturbate to numb out—pretending *it's* not part of the addiction—if I'm not with a guy. But that's such lonely, lonely sex."

"I always thought I was just a drunk," Dave says. He says

that after four times in detox for alcohol and drugs, the staff finally realized his core addiction was sex. And that he'd have a better chance to get sober once he stopped acting out sexually. "So here I am."

Jim, I hate these meetings. I want to touch the sleeve of your polo shirt. I want to watch your eyes, the color of limes.

"I'm Mary and I'm a flirt." Mary wears baggy sweats. Her hair is stringy, and she appears the least likely person to be a flirt. "That's all I do, flirt. Except I know I use this flirting to keep men away from me, you know, to prevent them from knowing the *real* me. And I also think it's manipulative, because isn't flirting just trying to control men and make them want me? Plus, I don't tell my husband about the flirting. And isn't keeping secrets what addiction's all about?"

"I'm Loni. I used to think all these men were attracted to me and asked me out all the time and wanted to seduce me because I'm pretty and sexy and fun to be with and all. Now I know they were after me because I'm available."

Jim turns to Loni. He watches her with the same intensity he must have watched the woman in the Camaro, the same way he watched me at the beginning of the meeting.

Jim?

I will myself not to look at him. I will myself not to watch him. I lean forward slightly and focus on one brown linoleum tile on the floor. Marking it into quadrants with my eyes, I begin to count white specks, determined to calculate the total number. I lose count.

I begin again. I must. The linoleum is old and chipped, probably made with asbestos fibers. I take a deep breath, hoping to be struck with lung cancer right on the spot.

I already feel winded, as if I'm crashing from space, no longer buoyed by Jim's gaze, no longer buoyed by the high of imagining us running away together.

The rush and clamor of addiction flatten.

I feel absolutely still.

And in this stillness I see that if I could be the woman in the Camaro, or if Loni could be, then *all* women, to Jim, could be. All women are the woman in the Camaro.

Except Jim can't see the real woman in the Camaro because all sex addicts are blind.

"Hey, I'm still Linda and I'm still a sex addict. Or love addict."

At the sound of Linda's voice I glance up. Tonight she wears her hair in a long braid draped over a shoulder.

"I think I'm really figuring things out," she says. "About how I almost *had* to grow up to be a sex addict. I mean, my father was one. He never actually *touched* my sister or me, but it was like this covert incestuous stuff because he always watched us—first my older sister, then me. He always asked us about our periods and was curious about our bodies. He'd ask about our boyfriends and dates, wanting to know how the guys kissed us, how we liked sex. And he'd walk around naked. Or like in our swimming pool, he'd pretend to be playing, but he'd pull down the straps of our bathing suits."

Linda picks up the end of her braid and holds on to it. "Of

course, it won't do any good to sit around blaming him," she adds. "I know I've got to take responsibility for myself now."

This September evening the cinder-block basement is cooler. Still we scuff our feet, restless on metal folding chairs. Time feels static, although it can't be, in that time must also be inclusive. I think about what Linda said. None of us would be here if time didn't encompass the past. Linda's right: all of us evolved from addictive families. If we don't share the same addiction as our parents, our grandparents, our great-grandparents, then we developed others. I inherited my father's vision of a world of sexual objectification. Just like Linda. Linda and me. Men and me. I think about all the men I selected because they sexualized me, just as I objectified them.

"I'm Sheila and I'm sexually anorexic."

I shift in her direction, away from Jim, knowing if I move my eyes so much as one-sixteenth of an inch, he will float into my field of vision. I try to focus on Sheila, surprised she said the word *sex*, surprised she labeled herself at all. Nervous, she tugs a clump of hair, the hair ends a demarcation line for her face: above the line her eyes seem scared, while below her mouth is angry.

"I don't want to be here," she says. "I have to say I've always been really put off by you people." She folds her arms across her chest as if we might contaminate her. "I'm in treatment right now. . . ." She looks at Linda and me. "And a couple of weeks ago I told the group on the unit I'd never been in a relationship. And in a way this's true, except there was a man once who must've been a sex addict. I mean, he wanted sex all the time, wanted to have it with *me* all the time. And *that's* what I felt high on, if you could call it that, that when he wanted it, I could say no. And the more he'd beg, the more powerful and, in a way, in control I felt, watching his need, when he's out of control.

"But my therapist says I'm sexually anorexic, and that it's all part of the same disease. And I guess I've heard that slogan, 'One hundred eighty degrees from sick is sick.' But . . ."

She takes a deep breath. She bites her lower lip. "But who am I kidding?" Her voice is low as she exhales. "I mean, take one look at me." As she says this, she is the one who looks up, straight at us. "I'm *just* as out of control. With food. And I'm *scared* to have sex. I don't want anyone to see me. Because I'm *fat*.

"And besides, my therapist told me that he thinks every fat cell in my body is just an unshed tear. Kind of like what Brad said about depression. Except it's so hard to cry. I'm afraid once I start, I won't stop. So I eat and eat and now I just feel like I'm hiding my real self behind all this *fat*. I'm scared if I lose it I'll *see* something.

"There's one more thing," Sheila says. "Last night a bunch of us were fooling around." She looks over at Jill, who's in the other group. "And someone asked me to dance." She flushes. "I mean, it was just a girl. But, you know, that's the first time in my life anyone asked me to dance."

As Sheila spoke, and before when Linda spoke, I felt their words. Now Sheila and Linda are still. And in this stillness

how easy, finally, to see the simplicity of the struggle. It
needn't be as complicated as I'd imagined. Just a few words:
We are all addicts, are all in this together. Together, we can
remove our masks. Here, we don't need to hide. Here, we are
all equal.

DAY
TWENTY-TWO

TO MY SLEEPING EARS the sound registers as sharp, yet muffled. I listen for it to be repeated. I want to fall back to sleep, but I can't. Fainter sounds now reach me from the bathroom. Jill is not in bed. The bathroom door is closed. I get out of bed, tap, then open the door.

Jill has thrown a bottle of body lotion. Yellow cream is splattered across the tiled walls and floor. Shards of glass are in the sink, on the closed lid of the toilet, in the tub, on the floor. The top of the bottle has rolled beneath the sink.

Jill sits on the edge of the tub. Her mouth is tight with rage, while her cheeks are flushed. She breathes sharply. All

the curlers she wears to bed have been yanked and tossed in
the tub. She holds a shard of glass in her hand.

"What is it?" I whisper.

"I am so fucking angry," she whispers back.

"Why?"

"*I don't know why.* I feel like taking a hammer and smash-
ing every fucking pink tile in this bathroom."

Something that happened at the zoo? I wonder. The elephants? That girl in pigtails who resembled Jesse? I look at
the shard of glass.

"Well, you want me to help you clean this up? You know
what the staff's going to think if they see all this glass."

"What—that I'm trying to off myself? If I really wanted to,
which I don't, I wouldn't do it here."

I pull on my sneakers and pick up Jill's slippers. To clean
up the glass, I get a T-shirt and one of the baggies Jill uses for
curlers.

With the shirt wrapped around my hand, I crouch beside
the sink and the toilet, sweeping the slivers. I brush glass
along the edge of the wall and the base of the tub. It makes
scratching noises against the tile.

"I think I just wanted an oil tanker full of vodka," Jill says.

She means *this* is why she got angry and smashed the bottle of lotion.

I take the broken glass from Jill's hand, drop it in the baggie, then scoop up the rest. I dampen toilet paper and scrub
the floor for the last traces, then wipe the lotion off the walls.

"Actually, I really wanted to fuck this man I saw at the zoo."

"Yeah, but after, you'd just have to find another one." I

dump the paper into the toilet and flush. "Aren't you sick of this? Christ, I'm getting so sick of this. Why don't we make a pact and just stop? Cold turkey. Right now."

I have a long-standing prediction for myself: if I don't quit the addiction I will end up abandoned by everyone, a homeless person. At one point I had even staked out my personal subway grate in New York City and imagined living over it in a refrigerator carton. "I mean, you want to be doing this when you're seventy?" I ask.

"I've been doing it my whole life," she says. "Like Sheila says about food: 'There's never enough.' It's true. It's just that . . ." She turns on the faucets and splashes water on her face. Without looking at me, staring at the water rushing down the drain, she says, "So, you want to know what really happened when I left here?"

"I thought you got drunk and picked up some guy."

"Except that . . ." She grips the faucets. "I *tried* to. But it didn't work."

"What didn't?"

"This asshole dork of a man said he wouldn't have sex with me. He turned me down cold. No man has ever turned me down. He said I was too drunk and didn't know what I was doing. And he just left me sitting there at the bar all by myself. I was mortified."

She turns off the faucets. Water drips from her fingers and chin. I nudge a towel into her hand.

"I think it's possible for that to be seen as a kind of compliment," I say. "I mean, I know that's a stretch—"

"A *compliment*?" She flings the towel into the sink. "I took it as a full-scale total rejection of every cell in my entire body."

"Maybe he respected you."

"*Respect?*" Jill shivers. "That is a horrifying thought."

"Don't you ever want love, respect, a family—"

"I've already 'done' family."

"Well, maybe you could limit yourself to love and respect, then—"

"Like who even knows where my stupid sister Jesse is?" she interrupts me. She picks up the towel and drapes it over her head. "Except, you know, there is this one really clear picture I have of her." Her voice is muffled through the terry cloth. Jill tells me she remembers a white shirt, the back of a white shirt, shoulder blades, all moving away from her, until Jesse is gone.

Jill yanks off the towel, sweeping her bangs straight up from her forehead. "But what really gets me about that guy in the bar is that I didn't even *want* to have sex with him. I was doing him a favor."

She walks past me into the bedroom. I follow her and slide under the covers.

I am about to close my eyes when I understand the significance of Jill's story about the man in the bar. "But you came back here," I say, sitting up. "I mean, because of that man. Because he *wouldn't* have sex with you, you came back. So you *must* want something different. So that's good."

"You are so damn blind," she says. "I came back here to fuck Gabriel."

And then, even though I don't know whether to believe

her or not, I know it is over. Even as I don't know how to define the word *it*, I know it is over. It is over. With Jill. With Gabriel. All of them. I am too enraged to speak. There is nothing to say anyway. It is over. I can never allow myself to feel this way again. Simply, it is over.

DAY
TWENTY-THREE

WE ARE BROUGHT OUTSIDE to play volleyball in a small field behind the hospital. No one is interested. Nancy tries to drum up enthusiasm, but we're all sprawled on the grass, angry, restless, exhausted, lethargic. She says we've got to be more active. Learn to play, learn to have fun. Learn to play and have fun without men, she jokes. No one laughs.

I am way too angry to laugh. I am still too angry to speak to Jill. At weigh-in, when I knew she could hear me, I told Nancy I would leave the unit unless they switched my room-mate. At breakfast, when Jill placed her tray on my table, I moved to another table. It's not that I'm jealous, not the way I felt when I ran away from the unit. I am angry because of *how* she told me. And why. She did not reveal her secret as confession or apology.

"Jill," Nancy says now. "Why don't you be a captain? And Sheila. How about you? Choose sides."

In jeans and work shirt, Nancy stands by the net holding a volleyball. Her round sturdy face is all business.

Jill, who acts as if last night never happened, says, "If I break so much as one millimeter off a fingernail, I'm going to sue the hospital."

"Give it a rest," Nancy says.

As we begin to play, something I can only call *rage* slams the volleyball across the net every time I hit it. In fact, it's not "me" playing; rather, a woman called *rage*. The sun is at my back, and I feel as if violent sunrays are striking my shoulders, my elbows, my palms, pounding the ball. Briefly, I think of Forrest. The basketball. The sun. Maybe the volleyball is my own planet—not the sun—but a cold hard lightless moon. I spike the ball across the net straight at Jill. I am all energy: galvanized, directed.

I sense Jill understands what I am doing. If she is angry, she pretends otherwise, would not want me to know I affect her. Her smile is distant. Her tough, wiry arms protect her from my rage. She is my only focus. All the other women are blurs of color and movement, no distinction. When it is my serve, I smash the ball in Jill's direction. She misses. The ball bounces to the ground. I serve again. And again. My left palm is red and sore. It is warm to the touch and the skin is stinging by the time I finish serving.

Jill's team beats mine, but I don't even care. The moment

the game ends, I am running from the field back to the hospital. To pack. I can't just switch roommates, I must leave. Right now. I can't see Jill again. Ever. I can't be, yes, seduced into liking her again.

Then, as I reach the edge of the field and my feet hit the parking lot—this, while running away from Jill—it's as if I glimpse an image of Jill's sister. My feet slow. My mind slows. As it does, I hear Jill's words from last night, maybe the only honest words—a truth—she ever spoke to me, that image of her sister's back—the white shirt—her sister's shoulder blades—her sister, walking away. Her sister, disappearing.

And *that* is the ancient moment from which Jill can't awaken or grow. If only she would. If only she'd search for her sister, talk about her, her family, then *she*, Jill, wouldn't have to run away. From here. From me. From her life.

I whirl around. Jill, laughing, is walking back with Linda and a couple of other women. I retrace my steps until I stand in her path. Her eyes are dark with dare and suspicion. Her lips are slightly parted as if already forming words to slam me out of her life. She has done all this on purpose; she has willed this encounter.

"Me, other women—to you, we're *all* your sister," I say. "That why you have to push us away from you? Scared *we* might leave you like she did?"

"Oh, go talk to Ted. Frankly, I don't need this anymore." Jill has removed her rings and bracelets in order to play volleyball. In the sun her pale, bare arms look perishable. A condition I see as incurable. "I'm getting out of this place," she adds. "This time for good."

She turns and heads toward the hospital. Heat rises from the pavement. Asphalt steams around her ankles as if the city of Atlanta has turned to vapor. The sheer strength of Jill's insurgent will allows her to move, to walk, to leave, to force others to leave, while she remains seemingly unscathed. Watching her walk away, I now suspect *she* is the real vagabond sister, not Jesse. Jill, I suspect, is really the sister who ran away—but from her true self—maybe even long before Jesse left their house.

I lean against the doorjamb watching Jill pack. I sense tiny tremors of anger against the wood—uncertain if they're hers or mine. I can't stop watching her, as if I am to be the only witness at an accident.

Before, when Jill stormed off the unit, she tossed her stuff into suitcases. Now her anger is slow and deliberate. She neatly folds dresses, blouses, skirts. She carefully places cosmetics in baggies. She collects dirty socks, underwear, T-shirts from the floor. Using tissue paper, she wraps white sandals, patent-leather heels with red bows, and places them in her suitcase. The more delicately she folds her clothes, the more incensed I become until I think I am breathing rage.

She zips her suitcases and surveys the room. "If I've forgotten anything, feel free to keep it." Her smile is dismissive.

"I don't want anything from you."

"That's a lie."

I grip the doorjamb as she shoves her suitcases toward the door. I refuse to step aside. "So why don't you tell me why you *really* returned?" I say. "I mean, you'd come all the way back here just to fuck Gabriel?"

Her perfume, in the closeness of our bodies, smells darker, more seductive, more dangerous. "Yes." She says the word as harshly as possible, then kicks her suitcase to the side in order to step around me.

I know once she disappears down the hall, she disappears forever. I know, even if I want to, I'll never be able to find her.

I put my foot out, blocking the suitcase.

"Then you must've fucked Gabriel only 'cause you're scared to get better. You must've fucked him 'cause if you let yourself get close to me, or any of us, you might get better."

She picks up two suitcases and kicks the third around my foot and down the hall. "Jill." My voice weakens. To her back I whisper, "I know why you asked Sheila to dance. And I know you know what that meant to her."

Slowly she turns. Her lips barely part as she speaks. "It was a joke."

"I don't believe you."

"Don't care for us so much. You know? Don't bother. Why would you care?"

"Because you don't have to do this. If only you'd talk—"

"There's nothing to talk about. I'm perfectly fine."

"Fine—with those gray teeth."

She turns and continues to walk away. With the weight of

her luggage, her shoulder blades strain against her shirt. When she reaches the end of the hall, she drops the cases and sits on one to wait for the elevator. From this distance, she appears like a little girl perched on that bulging suitcase. From this distance, I no longer feel her danger or dare.

Don't care for us.

She did not say "me." Rather, "us." Meaning, her and men. She understands she is like the men to whom I'm addicted. Inconstant. Inaccessible. Unavailable. Running away so we can't get close.

My breath slows. I release my grip on the doorjamb. I must let go, I think.

Jill kicks her suitcases inside the elevator.

Don't care for us. Now, watching Jill leave, it is my own sister, I see. Running away, disappearing.

Except I can leave, too. What difference does it make who, technically, walks out the door first?

I retrieve my blue canvas bag from the closet. I haven't brought much and begin to jam my stuff into it. A few T-shirts. Two extra pairs of shorts. Underwear. Socks. In the bathroom I collect toothpaste, toothbrush, a bar of soap, deodorant. In a few minutes I'm finished. I wish it had taken longer, and I think about unpacking just so I can repack, to emphasize my statement.

No one is here to witness my statement.

I am alone.

It is my choice: I can slip the strap of the suitcase on my shoulder and walk out the door. Or not.

But I already left the unit once. I already tried that. From whom will I be walking away? Jill is gone. Gabriel is gone. They are all *out there.*

I will be walking away from no one. No: I will be walking away from Ted. I will be walking away from Linda. I will be walking away from my life.

If I walk out the door, I will not be alone. My addict will still be stitched to my heart.

I sit on the bed. The phone is beside me. In order to forget Jill, I can call Gabriel.

I pick up the phone and begin to dial his number. Halfway through, I depress the plunger. Yet I grip the receiver, holding it as if it's his hand.

I release the plunger. I am pressing numbers but realize I press more familiar ones. "Hi. You have reached Ted's confidential voice mail. At the sound of the tone you will have two minutes to leave your name, your number, and a message, and I'll return your call as soon as I'm available. Thank you."

I hang up. I don't leave a message.

I pick up the phone again. On the second ring, Gabriel's answering machine whirs into action: "Have you ever thought that your dreams are answers to questions you don't know how to ask?"

If I announce my name he might answer. If I announce my name he might not. He might be home. He might not.

My dreams are usually nightmares.

Even if I hear his real voice I will only feel good for ten seconds after we hang up.

A wave of nausea presses my throat when I think about his voice. It is the nausea of overdose.

I let the receiver slide back into the cradle.

Then, again, I lift it. Again I dial Ted's number. "It's me," I say. "I just dialed Gabriel's number but didn't leave a message."

I unpack my suitcase. I return my T-shirts, shorts, underwear to the dresser drawers. I put my toothbrush back in the bathroom and place my suitcase in the closet.

I go to the nurses' station and ask Nancy to bring me a dictionary when she comes to work tomorrow.

I return to my room. I sit on the bed. I listen, waiting for my breath to slow. My pulse to slow. Me to slow.

DAY
TWENTY-FOUR

TURQUOISE: *A blue to blue-green mineral of aluminum and copper, mainly* $CuAl_6(PO_4)_4(OH)_8.4H_2O$, *esteemed as a gemstone in its polished blue form.*

The dictionary says nothing about men cloaked in black like sorcerers with blue jewels, white feathers, and tobacco-colored skin scented with jasmine.

MAROON: *Dark reddish brown to dark purplish red.*

The dictionary says nothing about older men who smell of autumn wearing scarves draped around necks, drinking Manhattans with young girls in the Ritz-Carlton.

The dictionary does not sexualize ordinary items or substances—does not romanticize them. The dictionary does not decorate the world like a stage set for a seduction.

I must believe dictionary definitions are interesting enough. I must learn to deconstruct my addictwords, my addictimages, until I arrive at the core. Until I arrive at just *turquoise*, just *maroon*, just *feather*, just *sun*.

I must learn logic. Always, I believed that if I loved a dangerous man now in the present (and he loved me back), it would prove I loved my father in the past (and he loved me back). In order to conjure this illogical premise into truth, into fact, I used sorcerer crystals and cloaks of alchemy, brewed dark magic and plunged stakes into the heart of logic. I stirred potions and elixirs waiting for evidence of love to bubble to the surface. Now I must know that the true premise—that sex with a dangerous man is not love—is the only fact.

Maybe spirituality is to surrender to the force of these truths. To see rain, moons, suns as they *are*, not how they can be imagined with men. Maybe spirituality is to allow mornings and nights to teach me, not to control or create them, not to *be* them. If I can just be. If I can just accept being ordinary enough. More: if I can just *imagine* the ordinary. If I can be still enough without the addiction, still enough to hear the universe, what it can say.

If . . .

My pass to eat dinner with Andrew is for tomorrow night. I don't want to stop at Gabriel's.

My addict does.

If I stop . . .
If I don't . . .

Late afternoon I sit alone in the small sixth-floor lobby, watching the aquarium. Goldfish, fantails swish around miniature coral reefs, strands of seaweed, artificially colored rocks: a microcosm of the sea, but false. A snail sucks the side of the glass, its antennae stroking the water for signals, sounding the territory for danger. The fish swim back, forth, back, forth, up, down. No progress.

The afternoon sun angles low and casts wands of light through the water. For a moment the aquarium seems almost tropical. Water glitters. The red and blue coral lighten to almost natural colors. The antennae on the snail seem to sway more freely, sensing light. As sun continues to bloom through the water, membranes of the fins become transparent.

But the fish are still trapped behind glass.

DAY
TWENTY-FIVE

ANDREW AND I SIT across from each other in the OK Cafe. It's a down-home family restaurant with comfortable booths and paper napkins. Informal. Yet I feel as if I have reentered the world too suddenly. I am giddy and overwhelmed. Strange people. Loud voices. Laughter. Muzak. Babies crying. Dishes clattering. Waitresses swish by, their trays loaded with food. Too much food. I don't want to eat anything; no, I want to eat an entire chocolate cake, gorge myself until I am numb on sugar. In the next booth a man and woman sit beside each other whispering into each other's ears. My addict assumes they're having an affair. They're whispering about sex, about . . .

Stop, I tell myself. Be normal. Calm down. Control your thoughts. Change the channel. And start noticing *Andrew*. Pay attention to *him*. He's your *husband*.

I sit up straight in the booth. I take slow, even breaths. I'm nervous, my hands tremble, the menu shakes a little, but not enough for anyone to notice. I'm sure I look okay. Before I left the unit, Linda fixed my hair in a French braid. I borrowed pale pink lipstick from Nancy. I wore my T-shirt with the fewest rips. I feel washed, rinsed, waxed, polished. Trying. I want Andrew to notice this stronger woman I'm now slowly becoming. I look down at my body. Yes, heavier than when I entered treatment. Surely I'm heavy enough to be noticed.

I'm fine. I'll be fine. Slow down.

Andrew wears a new shirt, gray with white stripes. I wonder if he wore it for tonight. For me. Or maybe *he's* having an affair, maybe he bought it for . . .

Stop. Just focus on this moment. *Don't act crazy*. Pay a compliment to your husband. But how do you flirt with a man who's your *husband*? Do I say: *You look handsome. You look sexy*. My smile is forced. "Your shirt—it's very nice."

"I went shopping last weekend." He smiles. "Belk's was having a sale."

"I like the color on you," I say.

"Thank you. Glad you like it." He nods at the menu. "What looks good?"

Don't say: *Nothing*. Don't say: *I could eat an entire cake*. Appear calm. "Maybe a burger. I haven't had one since . . ." Since the night before I entered rehab. That thrown-together meal. "Actually, maybe I'll have the T-bone steak."

"I'm thinking roast beef," he says.

The waitress comes to take our order. I speak distinctly, calmly. Adultly. I can do this. This is something everyone in the universe does. I've just been out of circulation awhile. "And a glass of ice water with lemon, please."

"I'll have iced tea," Andrew says. "Sweetened."

Okay, everything's going well. So far, so good.

"Did you remember to feed Quizzle before you left the house?" I ask.

"Plenty of chips in her bowl," he says.

"I'm looking forward to seeing her," I say. "I mean . . ." What do I mean? I place my napkin on my lap and fold my hands on the table. "I mean, it'll be good to get home."

"Yeah, the house is quiet without . . ."

Without my tears, mood swings, loud silences. "You sure can't say that about the unit." No, that's not true, I now realize. Really, with Jill gone, the unit is quiet, is known, is dependable—compared to this restaurant with Muzak playing. Food everywhere. That couple. Odd to think I miss my room on the unit. The routine.

"You making friends there?" Andrew asks.

"Oh, sure. The women are very nice."

The couple in the booth nuzzle each other's faces. I must look away. Except outside the window couples cross the parking lot holding hands. *Why does everyone have to be so sexual?* Why can't everyone on the planet just be platonic? Friends.

Focus on Andrew. He's your husband. "How're classes going?" I ask.

"Pretty good. But, you know, too many papers to grade. And *Ulysses* can be tough for undergraduates."

The waitress brings our food. I don't want the T-bone steak, but I want Andrew to think everything's fine, so I'm determined to eat it. If I eat quickly, I'll be able to get rid of it sooner. No, I must eat slowly, calmly, normally. One hundred percent. I squeeze the lemon in the water and drink.

The Muzak plays "Strangers in the Night." The couple gazes into each other's eyes. The thin, tinny music tries so hard to sound romantic that I think I might cry. *Don't act crazy.* No one cries over Muzak.

Andrew! "How're the Braves doing?"

"Don't ask," he says. "They've lost five in a row. They're in last place."

"Bummer."

"It's a challenge to be a Braves fan. But I've been one since . . ."

Since you lived in Milwaukee, when they were the Milwaukee Braves. . . .

I carefully chew my food before swallowing. Steak. Baked potato. Garden salad. I wonder what the women on the unit are doing. I imagine Linda eating in the cafeteria without me. She and Sheila will sit together and wonder how *I'm* doing, out here. They'll want to hear all about it when I get back. I want to report "success" rather than "disaster."

"Your hair looks nice," he says. "It's different."

He noticed my hair! "*Thanks.* Linda, one of my friends, fixed it for me. It's called a French—" My mouth almost forms the word *kiss*. "*Braid*," I say.

After dinner, Andrew and I stand beside my car. It's almost dark, the breeze slightly cool. His hand brushes mine. The warmth seems to well up through my body. And suddenly I don't know how I can leave . . . how I can leave this man. This evening, this moment, I want to go home. With him. I want to see Quizzle. I want to be in my own house with this man who, yes, is my husband . . . even though I've never been sure what it means to have one. Enveloped in this early autumn breeze, this soft Georgia night, I don't want to be that other woman. *Her.* I want to be *me.* And I wonder if this is love, if this means I love my husband. I honestly don't know. Maybe I am only lonely.

"I'll see you home in a few days," he says.

Now is the time I *must* say one thing that's real, one thing that's honest to this man before he gets in his own car to drive away. Even if I'm not ready to tell him my truths, I have to think of at least one true sentence. "Are you nervous?" I say. "About me coming home."

He pauses before answering. Directness is new for him, too. "A little, I guess. You?"

"A little."

I take my car key from my purse and open the door.

He hugs me, briefly. I want it to last longer. I don't know how to tell him this. I also want him to protect me from this world: too large, too sexual, too dangerous.

I can only protect myself.

"Maybe we can schedule some family therapy sessions with Ted," I say. "Kind of work on things."

"Let's talk about it when you get home."

I slide behind the wheel. But do you want me to come home? Do you want to work on things? Do you want this marriage?

I follow the taillights of Andrew's car up the ramp to the interstate. Almost nine. An hour before I have to return to the unit. Earlier, before I left the unit, I was sure I would want to drive to Gabriel's after dinner. How could I not, once I was out? That's what I've done my whole life. Free time. Dead time. Fill it with a man. I'd thought I'd at least see where he lived, what his house looked like.

And now . . . I don't much care where he lives. But I am lonely driving out here in the world—Andrew's car heading north up I-75, alone toward home. I lose his taillights in the traffic. I could return to the unit. Talk to Linda. Return to the unit and call Andrew, tell him how much I enjoyed the dinner. Return to the unit and call Ted.

I pause outside Gabriel's house. I don't turn off the engine. Yet I don't know whether I am here to see him, here to say nothing, or here to say good-bye. Ordinary brick ranch. Ordinary street. Dogs bark. Pine straw around tulip trees. Spindly loblolly pines.

If it were the melodramatic, gothic me, I would use the word *gloam* to describe the evening. Really, though, it's just an ordinary night that's lit with the reflection of television sets flickering from plate-glass windows up and down the street. A television light in Gabriel's window.

That's all there is here.

Maybe I don't have to see him. Probably he, like every other man in Atlanta, sits in a La-Z-Boy recliner, a can of Bud in his hand, watching the Braves on television. The feather is probably not in his hair. From here, there is no scent of jasmine wafting out the window. Maybe he wears his turquoise earring. Maybe not.

In any event, turquoise decodes to a blue to blue-green mineral of aluminum and copper . . .

There's nothing for you out here, Ted once told me.

Ted is right: I projected love and spirituality onto Gabriel because I wanted him to be a spiritual person. I wanted to steal or borrow his because I have none of my own. I wanted a quick dose of soul. But Gabriel is only a bartender offering an alcoholic free drinks.

And now, all I want is to be back on the unit: safe, dependable, structured. And after that, home.

I put my car in gear and drive away.

DAY
TWENTY-SIX

TODAY, FOR EXERCISE, we are at a public swimming pool. I cling to the ledge, my neck bent, so no one can see I am crying. I am crying simply because I actually feel the water. I'm too unused to feeling anything real—even as I know all feelings can appear to be backward.

For example, when I'm fully in the power of that addict-woman, when I am *most* sick, I am, ironically, totally capable of swimming, going to parties, socializing: *being what appears to be normal*. Yes, all these years I've convinced not only myself but also others that my behavior is normal because, in the strength of the addiction, I can *seem* normal.

Now, however, when the addiction is receding, when I'm

in withdrawal, even though I'm getting better, everything
scares me and I appear to be a wreck. Except I'm not. I'm in
the process of becoming normal.

In this process I feel exposed, however. I feel as if Gabriel,
Jill, Rick, all of them, have been strip-mined from my body.
My addiction has been strip-mined from my body. Without
it, I am now able to feel water, a synonym for life.

I'm also crying now because last night in the restaurant I
couldn't. Not that I was sad last night. Rather, confused and
unsure. This world is beginning to look so sober, so different. I
don't know my place in it. I'm crying because I don't want
to leave the unit.

"What is it?" Linda says, swimming over to me. Her silky
eyelashes are flecked with water.

I grip the ledge of the swimming pool. "Who am I, without *it?*" I whisper.

"You."

"But I feel so . . . alone. That addict, you know, it's always
right there, first in line, in the front row."

"I know you—well—understood Jill." She pulls herself up
until her elbows rest on the ledge. "But maybe, for starters,
we can be friends."

Yes, I think. Once I learn to care what happens to Linda,
then I can care what happens to me. Once I see the real me, I
can be with the real you.

Without my addict, I *won't* be alone . . . just as Ted always
told me. That is the point. It is *with* my addict I am alone.

"But like last night with Andrew," I say, "that was so
strange. I don't even know if that was me in the restaurant. I

was trying so hard to be perfect. The way I thought he'd want me to act—adult, normal. I mean, I wasn't my addict. But I don't know if it was *me*, either."

"Ted would say that to be 'you' it's just a matter of being emotionally honest about feelings. And not keeping secrets."

I nod. "I've been keeping a secret since I entered rehab," I say. "Can I show it to you when we get back to the unit?"

From the bottom of my suitcase I retrieve Forrest's scarf and explain its significance to Linda, who sits on Jill's old bed. I stand by the window and hold it up to the light. The edges are frayed, the material worn and thin in the middle, the section I once thought kept the nape of my neck warm and safe. I press it to my face. No autumn scent. If anything, it has a slightly antiseptic smell of the unit—as if it, too, needed to be here.

At one corner is a small moth hole. I poke my finger through, widening it. And wider still, until I have severed threads and the hole is about the size of a quarter.

My panic feels watery, just behind my knees, even with this small act of betrayal toward Forrest, toward the addiction. Yet when I return home I must also destroy the letters and mementos I save in the wood lavender box. I must rip the pages from the books of fiction. I must cut men's faces from photographs.

But this is so scary. I comb the ripped threads of the scarf together as if I can stitch the hole shut.

No, I can't stitch it shut. With my forefingers I tug the material harder. The hole widens. I tug harder still until I

grip the edges in my fists. It rips. Forrest, you must go now. I
don't even know whether you're still alive.

"I can't leave here with it," I say to Linda.

What is a ritual? Now I need a good sorcerer's powers to
combust the scarf.

"How about the dumpster?" She nods her head toward
the window. Below is a delivery entrance to the hospital and
beside it are two dumpsters.

I had envisioned setting the scarf on fire or cutting it into
shreds. But the idea of the dumpster seems right. The scarf
isn't worth the purity of fire.

Linda and I go downstairs to the rear of the hospital. I toss
the scarf into the dumpster while Linda claps her hands and
cheers, as if I've just done something amazing.

DAY
TWENTY-SEVEN

TODAY IS THE LAST group therapy session for several women on the unit, including Linda and me, before we leave tomorrow. Ted suggests exercises to help us note the progress we've made since starting recovery. He passes out a handout entitled "Emotional Vocabulary." On this list we are to put X marks next to five words that describe how we felt when we entered treatment, and checkmarks next to five words to describe our feelings now.

AFRAID	SEDUCTIVE	FRUSTRATED
CONFIDENT	MIXED-UP	DISCOURAGED
COMPLACENT	CONFUSED	EXHAUSTED
WORTHY	FRIENDLY	HURT

PEACEFUL	SUSPICIOUS	DISTRUSTFUL
OKAY	CAPABLE	HOPELESS
HORRIFIED	IMPORTANT	UNIMPORTANT
UPSET	AFFECTIONATE	HUMILIATED
EDGY	ADVENTUROUS	REJECTED
OUT-OF-CONTROL	SECURE	JEALOUS

Words. I think back to the woman I was when I entered treatment, that morning after acting out with Rick. I'd packed a razor blade in my suitcase. I'd lied on my admittance forms. I'd "fallen in love" with Gabriel scant hours after arriving. And I put a lot of energy into obsessing about Jill. Which are the best words to describe *that* me? I reread the list. I put an X beside *out-of-control. Seductive. Hopeless. Humiliated.* Four words. One more. *Mixed-up.* Yet I also know I was afraid, horrified, edgy, confused, frustrated, discouraged, hurt, unimportant, rejected, and jealous.

Which words describe me now?

Scanning the list, I am startled. Except for just a moment ago, when I recalled acting out with Rick, I suddenly realize I haven't thought about him for hours. Or Gabriel. I am shocked. This must be the longest I've ever gone in my life without thinking about a man.

So the first two words I choose are *okay* and *peaceful.* I feel *friendly* as well. *Capable? Important? Secure?* No. Not yet. For now, I can claim only three sober words. But I hope that soon, if I remain sober after I leave the hospital, I will begin to feel some of these other words as well.

"Let's try another exercise," Ted says. "Word association.

I'll say a word and, anyone, just call out the first thing that comes to mind. We'll start with words your *addict* would select. So if I say 'animal,' what word comes to your addict's mind?"

"Black stallion," Linda says.

"Snakes."

"Leopards," I say.

"Okay," Ted says. "If I say 'nature.'"

"Moonlight," I say.

"Sunsets."

"Walking along the ocean."

"Everything in nature reminds me—reminds my addict—of a man," Linda says.

"Thunderstorms."

"One big blue moon."

"Let's try your sober minds now," Ted says. "What animals do you associate with sobriety?"

"My cat Quizzle," I say.

"Puppy dogs," Sheila says.

"What else?" Ted asks.

We all shrug and look around. "Okay," he says. "Keep working on this one." He pauses. "What about nature?"

"I don't 'do' nature without a man," Linda says.

"Maybe you could start seeing it as spiritual," Ted says. "Here's your assignment. All of you. When you leave here, go to the park and just think about *it*. About the sky, the grass, the trees." He smiles at us. "No men allowed."

To end group, Ted says he wants us to write short notes to give to each other, encouraging messages. He suggests we bring the notes home with us, small gifts, for when we're having a bad day. He hands out paper. "Just tell your friends what you admire about each other, what you'll miss."

My first note is to Linda. I write that I like to be with her because she seems so steady, so clear-headed, so safe. These are qualities I would depend on when I'm having a bad day. Or a good one.

Dear Sheila, I write next. *I admire you for what you said in the SAA group the other day. That took a lot of courage to be so honest. And courage is what you need when things are bad.*

As group ends, we pass out our notes. I collect the ones written to me and put them in my pocket. I am surprised by how pleased I am to receive notes from women: my new mementos.

Ted hands contracts to the women who are leaving, a promise we'll do whatever it takes to stay sober and safe once we're home. We must sign them before we leave the hospital.

After dinner, Ted raps on the door to my room. Even though I'll see him as an outpatient, he has come to say good-bye. "You made it," he says.

I've just begun to pack my suitcase. "Barely," I say.

"You did better than 'barely,'" he says. "You stayed. You didn't give up."

"Guess that would have been even harder."

"You plan to be in touch with Linda?" he asks.

"Probably."

"Is that a yes?"

I sigh and fold the STRANDED ON THE STRAND T-shirt with the ripped seam in the shoulder. I think I will throw it away when I get home. "*Yes,*" I say. "It's a yes."

"Good," he says. "What'll you do when Rick calls?"

"Not see him."

"How do you know?"

"Just the thought of him exhausts me."

"Guess the thrill's kind of gone," Ted says.

"At least for today."

"And Andrew? You thought the dinner went all right the other night?"

"He noticed my hair," I say. "That I wore it different."

"Good start," Ted says. "Now maybe you can show him who you are *in*side."

I put dirty socks in the suitcase. "He'll leave me."

"That might be true. But you have to trust yourself—and him—enough to try. Your marriage either has to be based on honesty, or else you'll continue to live a lie."

Yes, I must decide if I want Andrew for my family. A family. But *not* one like Forrest's—where wives don't see truths; where husbands lie.

"Change is so scary," I say. I place the notes the women wrote to me in group in my suitcase, saving them to read later. "Everything is."

"Even me?"

I stop packing and look at him. No disguises. Ted is always Ted. He is always emotionally available. "Guess my addict thought you were," I say. "But no, *I* don't think you're scary."

He asks if I signed the contract he gave me earlier. I hand it to him.

I will not act out with sex, food, alcohol, or anything else that could be considered a drug. I will not hurt myself no matter what I think or feel, including sadness, anger, or fear.

_____*Sue*_____
(your name)

"You're going to be okay out there," he says, nodding toward the window. "And I'll see you Tuesdays."

Late in the evening I walk down the hall toward the group room. The corridor and the walls in the lounge are decorated with a month's worth of art projects: crayoned outlines of our sober bodies, papier-mâché masks, representations of our Higher Powers, and photographs we cut from magazines to illustrate our futures. I collect my work to take home. I pull out the tack holding that photo of the isolated mountaintop. At the time I cut it out, I imagined *me* isolated and distant.

Now I wonder if I can see this scene some other way. If I traveled to that mountaintop in my mind, I think that now I could breathe deeply. A rush of cold air shocks my lungs, waking them. Wind gusts across my cheeks, flushed with real weather. I can finally feel that breeze I waited for, stranded on the Galveston jetty.

DAY
TWENTY-EIGHT

LINDA AND I STAND by the parking lot with our suitcases. Autumn sun warms my face, sun that's lost the fierceness of summer. Green drains from oak trees. Brown needles of loblolly pines film the grass.

"So I guess this's it," I say. The intimacy of good-byes scares me, and I hitch my suitcase strap onto my shoulder and stare across the lot toward my car.

"You going to go to SAA meetings?" she says. "Get a sponsor?"

"I think Ted says I have to. That he won't see me for individual sessions unless I'm also in a group."

Linda's hair is neatly braided around her head. Her pants

and shirt are swirled with earth colors. Her earrings are long loops of white bird feathers and black beads. I wear the same clothes in which I arrived here: khakis, T-shirt, untied Reeboks.

"They're not so bad," Linda says. "I heard about an all-women one that's starting Sunday nights. You want to meet and go together?"

I don't want to go. I never want to attend another meeting. "Okay," I say.

Linda sets her suitcase by her feet, not wanting a typical (hasty) addict good-bye. "We could eat some dinner at that Shoney's first." She nods her head up the parkway, her smile firm and sincere.

It can be this simple, I think, if I don't invest all my energy in caring for dangerous men, or caring for women like Jill, addicts who are impossible to care for.

I let the strap of my suitcase slide off my shoulder and down my arm. "Okay," I say. "Sure, yes, dinner."

"You know what I've had a huge urge to do ever since I met you?"

Oh, no, I think. She wants to hug me. "What?" I say.

"Tie your damn shoelaces."

I laugh. "You know what? I should probably learn to tie them myself."

We sit on the curb beside the grass berm where I waited for Gabriel. The once-red laces are frayed. I grip the ends and loop them together. Tying them seems to be my own personal limen, a threshold on a path to another, to one where I will be adult, to one where I take care of small details like tying laces, to taking care of myself, to paying attention—but not to men in silver trucks. Or maybe this simply means I've gotten it together enough to have my own shoelaces neatly tied.

"What do you think'll happen to Jill?" I ask. With the laces tied, the shoes feel snug and secure on my feet.

"Guess she'll keep going until she crashes. Hits bottom. Or decides to stop."

I nod. "In some ways I miss her."

Linda gouges a small pebble from the ground. It is brown. A few white streaks. But ordinary. Nothing unusual. She hands it to me.

"What's this for?"

"I like to collect stones from places where I go, places that mean something to me."

"Then don't you want to keep it?"

Her earrings brush her neck as she shakes her head. "You can keep it for both of us."

A charm, I think, but a safe one, a fetish for everydayness.

I put it in my pocket.

FIRST
DAY
OUT

THE PHONE RINGS.

Rick?

I've just gotten home from the hospital. When I first walked through the door, Quizzle, my cat, was overjoyed to see me. She skidded across the wood floors wanting me to chase her, a game she plays. I dropped my suitcase and ran after her up the stairs, down. Finally she let me catch her and stroke her chin.

When the phone rang.

Rick.

Andrew isn't home from work yet.

The sudden ringing in this quiet house, from which I've been absent so long, is jarring. This is the first phone call I've received in a month. Should I pick up the receiver? Maybe it's *not* Rick. Maybe it's Ted, seeing if I'm okay. Maybe it's Andrew, welcoming me home. Maybe it's Publishers Clearinghouse.

I sit on the bottom stair that leads to the living room. I stare at the yellow phone on the stand, about three feet from me. I want to answer it. I don't want to answer it. It keeps ringing. I could just pick it up and say hello. If it is Rick, I wouldn't even have to agree to meet him. No, I can't pick it up. Once I answer, once I hear his voice . . .

After at least ten rings it stops. My panic deepens. I know it was Rick. He will hate me for not answering. He will hate me if I never have sex with him again. He won't want me for a friend unless I fuck him.

That is the point.

Still, maybe it would be okay if I call him back and apologize. Maybe I should call Gabriel instead. I don't have to actually see either of them. I'd settle for knowing one of them wants me.

In my head I hear Ted's voice: *They don't want you. They want a fix. Hear what they're really offering.*

Nothing. Nothing that would be good for me.

I pick up the phone and carry it back to the stairs. I sit down again and stare at the twelve push buttons. My addict pleads for my fingers to dial Rick's number. Or Gabriel's.

"Hi. You have reached Ted's confidential voice mail. At the sound of the tone you will have two minutes to leave your name, your number, and a message, and I'll return your call as soon as I'm available. Thank you."

"Ted, it's me, Sue." I have two long minutes. So much time. Before, when I called him, I either hung up without leaving a message at all, or else I only used up about five seconds.

"I'm *home*," I continue. "I made it. I haven't acted out yet. I mean, I've only been home ten minutes, but still. I thought you'd be glad to know." I listen to the silence of his machine. I watch the second hand of my watch ticking.

"But *he* called. Just now. Rick. I *know* it was him."

Who else but an addict would know the second I walked in the door?

"*And I didn't answer the phone.*

"Can you believe it? Isn't that amazing? Are you shocked? I mean, this is the first time in my life I haven't answered the phone, because before I'd always hoped the caller would be a man, so how could I not answer? But now—"

A computer voice interrupts. "Your recording time is about to expire. Please finish your message within eight seconds."

While I consider what I most want to say in the remaining seconds, the line goes dead.

I redial. "Hi, you have reached . . ."

"Ted, it's me again. Sorry if I'm using up all your tape. But here's the thing I have to tell you." I slide from the bottom step down to the floor and lean against the wall. I bring up my knees, press my forehead against them, the receiver almost under my chin.

"I'm kind of freaking out," I say. "I mean, right now, even though it's me who didn't answer the phone, I'm feeling abandoned. I know Rick hates me. He'll never want to see me again. And if only I could call him back and flirt, *just a little*, just for a second or something, then he'd want me and I would feel so great.

"Okay, okay, I know, I can hear you telling me, that would be 'high,' not 'happy.' And I really, really know that awful feeling would come back again. I'd meet him. We'd fuck. Then I'd be *really* abandoned."

This is true. Not only would I feel abandoned by him, after, when he no longer needs me, but worse, I will feel abandoned by myself.

"Christ, I can't believe it. I think I actually learned something in the hospital after all." I explain to him what I'd just been thinking. "I mean, I can see how awful that would be to meet him. Because nothing would be different. It'd be the same shit, that awful, awful feeling like I was dying. I mean, I'd *feel* the way Pole Lady *looks*."

"Your recording time is about to expire . . ."

"Hi. You have reached . . ."

"Me again. Sorry if I'm bothering you. I think if I can just talk about this, figure this out, I won't want to call Rick back. You said talking about it makes it lose some of its power." Quizzle curls up beside me on the floor, and I run my fingers through her gray, silky fur.

"And, okay, what else would you be telling me right now?" I ask. "You'd say, 'Stay sober, stay safe.' You'd tell me to do whatever it takes to be safe. You know, back when I first started seeing you, that didn't make any sense to me. I heard those words, but I had no idea what you were talking about. Safe? I thought that meant I should be *with* Rick, because my addict felt so, well, high with him, that was the best I ever felt. Except, of course, now I know *those* feelings are all false.

"Gosh, I guess one day I'll probably relapse. That scares me. I don't want to. I want to have this absolutely *perfect* recovery program. I never want to have that awful needy feeling again, just needing a man *right now*. I never want to feel that again."

"Your recording time . . ."

"Hi. You have reached . . ."

"But I'm nervous about what happens if Andrew and I don't make it. Even though that dinner went okay, still, it was only *one* dinner. And I think he feels like I'm this noose around his neck. A burden. Like a dead weight. But if we don't make it, then I'm out there in the world all alone. With all those men.

"Yes, I know, I can hear you telling me that even *with* Andrew there were all those men. So marriage doesn't keep me safe. But I'm terrified to be alone. I've *never* been alone. Do you realize I've never been without a man for so much as one nanosecond? There's always been a man in my life. Usually more than one. I don't even know who I am without a man. Do you?

"Okay, I know you'd tell me I don't have to figure all this out right this second. Right now I just need to figure out today. Or this afternoon. Or this minute.

"But I guess I'm calling you because I can see that this recovery stuff might go on for a while." Quizzle's eyes are closed. She's purring. I scratch under her chin. "But it's really hard to change your behavior, isn't it? I mean, knowing you have to change—and then actually changing.

"Like right now, I have all afternoon with nothing to do. And tonight. Before, I could spend hours planning the next time I'd see Rick. Thinking about what to wear. Doing my nails. And now, what am I supposed to do tonight?

"Okay, yes, Andrew will be home soon, and we'll have dinner. Gosh, it's back to figuring out *dinners*. What *do* people eat every night? And I know I need to go to that Twelve-Step meeting later. There's one at eight o'clock. I can do that. And I can call Linda. But still, this is hard, isn't it?

"So I guess I'm really calling you because, well, I want you to know that I need . . ." That word. That word that's so hard to say.

Help.

"I want you to help me keep going."

I let the receiver slide back into the cradle. For now, I don't need to call Ted again. Finally, after talking so long, expending that energy, I feel calmer. My breath slows. I slow. For now I can sit here and be alone. Alone and safe. For now I can keep the contract, the promise I signed before I left the hospital. No urgent need to act out. No need to call Rick. No need to rush off. I rest my head back against the wall. Quizzle has fallen asleep. The house is still. Spotless, too, I now notice. I barely recognize it. Andrew must have cleaned the house just last night. The furniture is dusted. The floors vacuumed. It looks like a different home altogether from the one I left a month ago. Andrew has worked hard for things to look nice. To welcome me back?

Now it is me and Quizzle. And Andrew? All those other people who pounded my head like a junkie's migraine seem to be lifting from my consciousness. Evaporating. And in this quiet space normal sounds emerge. Quizzle's purr. Ted's voice. This quiet house. My new heart.

Andrew and I hug when he gets home. I hold him tight for a long moment. We smile at each other, shy. He's not sure who I am now; and I'm not sure who he is to me, now that I'm sober. We fix dinner together. I stir spaghetti in boiling water. Newman's Own tomato sauce bubbles in a pan. A red and white colander in the sink. Andrew toasts garlic bread in the Magic Chef oven and fixes salad. Waiting for the food to cook, I wash clothes in the Maytag. Tide. Clorox 2. Downy fabric softener. I toss Ping-Pong balls across the floor for Quizzle to chase.

The timer goes off. The spaghetti is done. I lift the heavy pot from the stove and carry it to the sink. Pouring the water out my hand slips. The spaghetti misses the colander and it all slides right in the sink. Some strands coil into the drain.

Andrew's back is to me. He's stirring the sauce and doesn't notice. I am devastated that I have ruined dinner—that Andrew might think I'm still a total failure—and for a moment I am almost paralyzed.

Then I begin to grab handfuls of steaming spaghetti. It burns my fingers, but I continue to scoop it up and throw it into the colander. Even though the sink doesn't have a garbage disposal, I shove a few remaining strands down the drain. I turn on hot water and hold the colander under the faucet, cleaning the spaghetti as best I can. Then I turn on cold water to soothe my skin.

Carefully now, very carefully, I slide the spaghetti into a serving bowl. I pour on the tomato sauce, mix it with a spoon, and top it with grated Parmesan cheese.

It looks fine, I think. I place the bowl in the middle of the kitchen table and smile.

We watch the Braves while eating. Tom Glavine strikes out the side. Skip Caray riffs on the game. When Ron Gant makes a great catch in left field, Andrew beams.

Good. The game is a good distraction. Andrew hasn't noticed anything wrong with the spaghetti.

I'm feeling better.

"The house looks nice," I say. "I can tell you really worked hard cleaning it."

"I called an electrician to install that ceiling fan in the kitchen, too," he says.

"That's great," I say. All summer I'd meant to attend to this; now it's autumn, but at least we'll be ready for next summer.

Even with the small calamity over the spaghetti, this must count as a fairly successful meal. And I can smile at Andrew—not weeping over food, as usual. In fact, I eat everything. Clean my plate. My pulse is normal. I don't watch the clock to determine whether it might be time. To rush off. To meet some man.

I tell Andrew I'll go grocery shopping tomorrow. Brazenly, I add, "Maybe I'll even check a cookbook first, make something like a real meal!"

"*That* would be different," he teases.

"I'll wash up," I say, meaning the dishes. "Want to keep me company?"

He stands beside me at the sink. "I heard about this job," he says. He lifts plates from the rack and dries them. He tells me that a faculty member at a nearby college (not the one where he teaches) is going on sabbatical in January. Since the position is only for one semester, Andrew thinks they won't necessarily be hiring someone with a Ph.D., that my master's degree in creative writing would probably be enough. "I thought you might like to try."

Try something practical, he means. A job. But I've never taught. So much responsibility. Yet I *have* held responsible positions in the past, such as on Capitol Hill and at that historical preservation organization. "But I don't really have any experience teaching," I say.

"I would help you prepare."

"I guess it wouldn't hurt to apply." Trying new things is scary. But I have to fill up time. I also have to learn to feel good about myself, be proud of accomplishments. A reason I haven't worked for a few years (even though Andrew has wanted me to) is because of exhaustion. The exhaustion of living a double life. I quit the career world to work the job of a full-time addict. Now I'll have the energy to work. Make real friends. Cook dinner. Life.

"I can give you the phone number to call for an interview,"

Andrew says. He puts the last plate away. I turn out the light in the kitchen and follow him down the hall toward his study. "And—let me show you—I have some books you can look at."

"Could we do it later?" I say. "I hope it's all right, but there's this meeting tonight. One of those Twelve-Step groups. Ted thinks I should go. You know, to have that contact, since I just got out."

I wish I could tell him how close I came to answering the phone this afternoon. I wish I could tell him about Rick.

"I guess I thought you were okay now," Andrew says. "And if you get this job . . ."

Being "okay" is about more than working, I want to say. But Andrew has turned from me to sit down at his desk. I want him to ask me about treatment. I want him to ask me why I needed to enter rehab in the first place. I want to tell him how hard it is to stay sober—probably much more difficult than teaching. But Andrew would rather talk about jobs, baseball, literature—because he's still afraid to know too much about me.

Yet I know Ted is right: it is also my responsibility to tell Andrew about Rick, all those men. *That* would get Andrew's attention.

"I think I've *got* to go to these meetings," I say instead. "But I'd like to talk more about the job tomorrow."

Returning home from the 12-Step group, I drive past the Rainbow Motel. I want to see it one last time. At night, the flashing neon rainbow arcs over a NO VACANCY sign. The parking lot is filled with cars. Dead leaves scud the surface of the lit pool. Of course, the young Indian girl isn't around. Still, I wonder if she would recognize me like this—dressed in sober clothes.

From here, at the edge of the lot, I can't see whether the light is on or off in room #213. It doesn't matter.

By the time I reach home, the bedroom door is closed. I climb the stairs back to my room on the second floor. While Andrew and I may be closer, I guess we aren't ready to sleep in the same bed together. Still too many lies. I must tell him my truths, but I'm not ready yet. I can't change all my behaviors in a month. All I can do is keep working on myself, keep moving forward, keep trying.

That's what Linda at the 12-Step group told me this evening after I recounted my first hours at home, the near disasters. Still, it felt good to speak honestly about my fear that Rick might call again. It felt good to ask for help, to say I need the support of the group. And everybody cheered when Linda picked up her thirty-day sobriety chip: *Clean and serene for 30 days.* I'm looking forward to picking up my own thirty-day chip. I want everyone to cheer for me, too. I think I'll make it.

Now alone in my room I must concentrate on one day at a time. One night at a time. I can't spend tonight planning for next Thursday at noon. I can't think about what Rick is doing right this minute. I can't think about Gabriel. I must figure out something different. I must fill up my own time.

From the lavender box I remove letters, faded flowers,

crumpled cocktail napkins. From the bathroom I scoop up bottles of nail polish and the remaining Gillette single-edged razor blades. I begin to toss stuff in a garbage bag. But I'm not ready to part with everything. I put a few books and letters back in the box.

I also decide to save that photograph of me by the boardwalk in New Jersey—a tangible reminder of that girl I was. It's as if I want to be able to take her hand, hold it, reassure her that it's all right for us to get better. Maybe, the more sober I become, I'll want a reminder of where I've been.

Love is here every day! Before, "here" was a bar, a motel, a boardwalk. Now I must learn that love is where I carve out my own life.

I sit on the floor, holding those notes the women wrote to me in our last group therapy session. I have waited until now to look at them. One by one I read their good-byes and sincere best wishes for a safe and sober future. I read about how much they will miss me. *I know you can stay sober. Hope to see you again in 12-Step groups,* they write.

I must find comfort in these ordinary messages, normal people, everyday things. I must accept that the ordinary isn't boring, that the everyday can even be spiritual.

I wonder how all those women are tonight. Some are home. Others remain on the unit. The unit. I miss it. I miss the sound of women's voices. Ted's voice. These are the sounds of safety I must now imagine guiding me.

The small stone Linda gave me is on the table next to my

bed. Beside it, I set the papier-mâché mask. I tape that photograph of the mountain, the one I cut out of a magazine in
art therapy group, to my wall. Next to it I tape the large
sheet of paper with the outline of my body. And right where
I drew it, right where it should be, filling my chest, is my red
crayon heart.